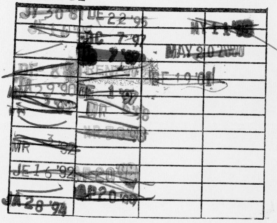

The Master Musicians Series

BARTÓK

Series edited by
Sir Jack Westrup MA, HonDMus(Oxon), FRCO
Professor Emeritus of Music, Oxford University

THE MASTER MUSICIANS SERIES

BARTÓK

by Lajos Lesznai

Translated from the German by Percy M. Young

With eight pages of plates and
music examples in text

London
J. M. DENT & SONS LTD

Originally published under the title BÉLA BARTÓK
© Lajos Lesznai, 1961
First published in Great Britain 1973
© This translation J. M. Dent & Sons Ltd 1973

Made in Great Britain
at the
Aldine Press · Letchworth · Herts
for
J. M. Dent & Sons Ltd
Aldine House · Albemarle Street · London

ISBN: 0 460 03136 8

Preface

Béla Bartók is one of those composers about whom many articles and books, in various languages, were published in their lifetime—a fact that shows how soon it was realized that his music was of great significance.

The first important book about Bartók was perhaps Edwin von der Nüll's *Béla Bartók: ein Beitrag zur Morphologie der neuen Musik* (Halle, 1930). Nüll, however, made virtually no reference to Hungarian folksong and its influence on the art of Bartók. Next came E. Haraszti's *Béla Bartók: His life and works* (Paris, 1938). This author was a Hungarian, but Bartók protested most energetically against the nature of the contents of his book. In 1939 Denis Dille published his *Béla Bartók* in Brussels. Although this is an interesting work it also makes no reference to the folk-music of Hungary.

It is impossible even to mention all the articles dealing with problems of Bartók's music that appeared in periodicals during his lifetime. It is, however, necessary to emphasize, as a factor of the greatest importance, that the real significance and essence of Bartók's music are only to be appreciated and understood in the light of Hungarian and probably other kinds of folk-music. Therefore a book on Bartók's music and his contributions to musicology is to be undertaken only after a thorough study of Hungarian folk-music.

After the end of the Second World War a considerable growth in books and essays about Bartók took place. Among the important works were Halsey Stevens, *The Life and Music of Béla Bartók* (New York, 1953, 2nd ed. 1964), Jürgen Uhde, *Béla Bartók* (Berlin, 1959) and Bence Szabolcsi, *Béla Bartók, Leben und Werk* (Leipzig, 1961). Of the many other works dealing with special aspects of Bartók's work which appeared in Hungarian, French, English, German and other languages, it will here suffice to mention two. Of particular interest are Dr Hans Ulrich Engelmann, *Béla Bartóks Mikrokosmos* (Würzburg, 1953), and Jürgen Uhde, *Bartók—Mikrokosmos* (Regensburg, 1955).

Very many of the biographical details in the present work are founded on special inquiries among those who knew Bartók personally. Of those who helped me in this way a large number are, alas, no more with us. Having attempted to lay the foundations of a factually accurate biography I have further tried to find the connection between the life and works of Bartók and the pattern of the times in which he lived. Beyond the music of the master the progress of his musicological development has also been explored.

If the reader feels that this book has given him a closer acquaintance with Bartók's music and made him aware of the composer's historical significance, the author will feel that he has achieved his purpose.

Budapest, 1973.   LAJOS LESZNAI.

Contents

Illustrations

Acknowledgments

Quotations from the following works are reproduced by kind permission of the publishers.
Editio Musica Zenemükiadó, Budapest:

Four Songs (Lajos Pósa)
Rhapsody for Piano and Orchestra
First Suite for Large Orchestra (Op. 3)
Two Portraits (Op. 10)
Two Rumanian Dances (Op. 8/a)
Three Burlesques (Op. 8/c)
Fourteen Bagatelles (Op. 6)

Boosey & Hawkes, Music Publishers Ltd:

Symphonic Poem, *Kossuth*
Second Suite for Orchestra (Op. 4)
Two Portraits (Op. 5)
For Children
Sonata for Two Pianos and Percussion
Second Violin Concerto
Divertimento for String Orchestra
Concerto for Orchestra
Third Piano Concerto

Acknowledgments

Extracts from the following are reproduced in the U.S.A. by kind permission of Boosey & Hawkes and in the rest of the world by kind permission of Universal Edition (London) Ltd:

Bluebeard's Castle
Allegro Barbaro
Piano Suite (Op. 14)
Second String Quartet
The Miraculous Mandarin
Dance Suite (Third Suite for Orchestra)
Piano Sonata
Out of Doors (*Night Sounds*)
Third String Quartet
Cantata Profana
Second Piano Concerto
44 Duos
Fifth String Quartet
Music for Strings, Percussion and Celesta

1   Origins and early schooling

Béla Bartók was born in the little township of Nagyszentmiklós in the district of Torontál, in Hungary. If one casts an
eye over the map one finds Nagyszentmiklós—which was
originally called Szerbnagyszentmiklós—about ten kilometres
from Marosch, near the town of Makó. It is situated on the
banks of the River Theiss between Szeged and Temesvár.
Now named Sânnicolaul-Mare, Béla Bartók's birth-place
today belongs to Rumania.[1]

The history of Nagyszentmiklós is sufficiently eventful to
merit closer consideration. After the end of the period of
Turkish rule, at the beginning of the eighteenth century,
Austria settled the neighbourhood as quickly as possible in
order to obliterate traces of the wars that had caused such
devastation. As a result of Austrian policy, German, Italian,
Spanish and French settlements were created, without much
consideration for the Hungarians. The poverty and waste that
followed the latest of the Turkish wars, as well as the appalling
aftermath of plague, further reduced the native population, so
that the Austrians sent in more settlers—Serbs, Germans and
Rumanians.

The many nationalities that established the character of
this strip of land, with their varied languages and customs,
made for favourable conditions for the development of
philological talent. It is not at all surprising that one of the
most important of Hungarian philological scholars—Miklós

[1] *See* reference to Rumanian folksong on p. 78.

Révai—was born in Nagyszentmiklós; and it would also seem not quite fortuitous that about 130 years later one of the greatest of musicians and most significant exponents of musical folklore—Béla Bartók—was born in the same place.

In the nineteenth century the population of Nagyszentmiklós comprised only Germans, Hungarians, Rumanians and Serbs. Each individual national group developed its own settlement, and all lived peaceably together. Because of its convenient situation so far as traffic was concerned—being at the crossroads of two important routes—Nagyszentmiklós soon became a thriving place. The weekly markets, as well as the Sunday markets for foodstuffs, held in the Market Place in front of the Town Hall, brought an increase in prosperity. Many strangers daily came to the town by the regular coach that linked Temesvár and Szeged, and stayed the night, or at least a few hours, in the tavern in the Market Place. This was a refuge from the notorious highwayman, Sándor Rózsa, who conducted his nefarious business in the neighbourhood of Nagyszentmiklós.

After the calamitous conclusion of the Hungarian War of Liberation (1848–9) a large number of government officials were sent to the neighbourhood. Representing the government and the ruling classes, they made German the official language. Stiff and rigid procedures in all branches of social activity, and the arid bureaucracy of officialdom, caused visible deterioration in the condition of a little town that had once been rich and lively. There was a slowing-down of construction work and trade, and there came a time when all the buildings on one street were up for sale. Moreover the hope of the inhabitants that the railway network would be completed was, for the time being, not fulfilled.

When this scheme finally could be implemented Nagyszentmiklós experienced a new period of economic prosperity. Several savings-banks, steam-mills, a brewery, plants for processing cattle foods, as well as other factories and businesses were established, and gave proof of renewed development in the community.

Soon after its foundation by Count Kristóf Nákó in 1799 the Agricultural College became also the cultural centre of Nagyszentmiklós. During the confused period after the War of Liberation its Principal was the Professor of Economics—János Bartók, grandfather of the composer. Under his purposeful leadership the institution grew in importance and through his dedicated work it became intimately bound up with the life of the entire Bartók family.

We can follow the history of the family back to Gergely Bartók, who was born in all probability in 1740 and died in 1825 in Borsodszirák. He married Mária Gondos, who was born in Borsodszirák in 1753, it is thought. She died in the place of her birth in 1820. Here the son of Gergely and Mária, János, was born in 1785. He died in Nagybecskerek in the 1870s. From his marriage with Katalin Bosznovics there were six children; the third of these, also János, lived from 1817 or 1818 until 1877. He died in Nagyszentmiklós. His wife, Matild Ronkovics (1825–85), was the daughter of a lawyer in Bánátkomlós. As already noted, this János was an economist and Principal of the Agricultural College in Nagyszentmiklós.

The name Bartók is frequently to be met with in Hungary, especially in the northern highlands, and in Transylvania. It can be taken as definite that the ancestors of Béla Bartók came from these parts—a conclusion to which the nickname 'szuhaföi' also points. Béla Bartók junior—son of the composer—indeed established the fact that this name came from a family tradition, indicated by the death certificate of his father and the birth certificate of his father and his father's sister.

János Bartók II in some way or other must have taken part in the War of Liberation, for afterwards he was obliged to go abroad. Between 1849 and 1852 he travelled in Germany,

Holland, Belgium and France, where he studied agriculture before returning to Nagyszentmiklós. Béla Bartók himself established evidence for these travels when he chanced to find the Visitors' Book of the Hungarian College in Berlin, and in it the characteristic handwriting of his grandfather. Although János Bartók had to provide for a large family he was among the more well-to-do citizens of his town, for his emoluments, as Principal, the support given to him by Count Nákó and his family, and (according to the custom of those days) certain payments in kind, represented a solid material foundation.

A legend about the Bartóks told how the highwayman Sándor Rózsa turned up one night with a group of confederates demanding lodging. János Bartók, it was said, received and entertained them so generously that Rózsa could do no other than show himself equally generous. In the grey light of morning he departed, without inflicting any kind of hurt on the household.

Béla Bartók, senior, the sixth child and third son of the nine children of János, was born in Dávidháza on 19th November 1855. Dávidháza was a settlement that belonged to Ujvár; it no longer exists. Nothing is certain about Béla Bartók senior's education. It is only known that he became a student at the Agricultural College at Magyaróvár; presumably, therefore, he had successfully passed through the six classes of the Grammar School. After the death of his father, which took place in 1877, Béla succeeded him as Principal of the Agricultural College in Nagyszentmiklós.

Bartók took an active part in the social affairs of his town, and was one of the leading figures in its musical life. He played the piano and was largely responsible for founding an orchestra. When it became clear to him that there was no cellist to be found in the town, he enthusiastically learned to play it himself. The direction of the orchestra was in the hands of a gipsy musician, and the first concert took place in the largest public house.

On 5th April 1880 Béla Bartók senior married a young teacher, Paula Voit, daughter of a tax official. Paula was born in 1857 in Turóczszentmárton, and at the time of her marriage she was an outstanding beauty. She was also highly educated and a great music-lover. It was said that as a pianist she had exceptional gifts. The first child of the marriage, Béla, later to become world famous as composer and musicologist, was born on 25th March 1881. On his birth certificate his full name was shown as Béla Victor János, and his god-parents were Victor Schreyer, a lawyer, and his wife Clementina (*née* Rillich), who lived in Rácznagyszentmiklós. Béla's sister, Erzsébet Clementina Paula, was born four years later, on 11th June 1885.

Although Béla was born with a strong constitution, he suffered a number of severe illnesses in infancy, which resulted in his developing into a particularly sensitive child. Thanks to the devoted care of his mother, however, his health was so much improved by the time he was five that it gave rise to no more particular anxiety.

Because of parental interest there was a good deal of music-making in the Bartók household. Precisely what music was played is no longer known, but it is reasonable to suppose that as well as the very ordinary polkas and *salon* music in vogue during the second half of the nineteenth century, popular Hungarian songs had a substantial place in the repertoire. These were art-songs (not folksongs) and at that time were enjoying renewed popularity.

In the Bartóks' house gipsy music was also often played. Béla listened to it most attentively, and it was obvious that its characteristic sounds engaged his full attention. When the orchestra founded by Bartók senior gave its first concert in the public house the audience went on eating, drinking and talking. While the orchestra was playing Rossini's *Semiramide* overture Béla, with childlike seriousness, spoke out to scold the adults for their behaviour.

Influenced by the music that he often heard, Béla gave his parents no peace, keeping on at them continually, until they promised that he should learn the piano. He had his first lesson on his fifth birthday, on 25th March 1886. About a month later he was able to play a piano duet with his mother for his father's 'Name-day' (the day of his patron saint).

Meanwhile his father's health grew worse, and it became necessary for him from time to time to take cures abroad. On one of these journeys—to Radegund, near Graz—he was accompanied by Béla. In 1888 Bartók senior was in such an enfeebled condition that he had to resign his post. On 4th August, at the age of thirty-three, he died. The so-called 'bronze-disease' (a disease of the liver) which he had contracted, was at that time incurable.

The death of his father began a new stage in the life of Béla's family. Acquaintances and friends in Nagyszentmiklós did all that they could to help the young widow, and a private school was started so that Mrs Bartók could earn her living. It used to be thought that the Agricultural College, in conjunction with the Nákó family, gave her a pension. Unfortunately this could not have been the case, because the college had now become a State Institute. Denied an allowance from this source Mrs Bartók was therefore compelled to return to teaching.

When he was seven, Béla went to the elementary school in Nagyszentmiklós, and was soon at the top of his class. He was barely eight when he left the fourth class with a glowing report. Mrs Bartók, however, was not satisfied. She was quite clear in her mind that the education that her son had so far had was by no means an adequate preparation for the kind of career she envisaged for him. She decided to leave Nagyszentmiklós and through her persistence was appointed to a post in the state elementary school in Nagyszőllős. According to her wishes Béla went through the fourth class curriculum once more, and in the next year entered the first class of the Middle School.

At that time Nagyszőllős was a very small town, which had no musical life of its own. Béla, therefore, was unable here to absorb any new musical impressions. Nevertheless the creative talent of the future composer first began to show itself at this time. He was nine when he began to compose—waltzes and polkas, as well as other conventional dances of the period, for piano.

When he was ten his mother took him to Budapest, to the distinguished teacher Károly Agghazy (1855–1918), who was a professor at the Conservatorium. Agghazy saw at once that Béla was highly gifted and would have been willing to accept him as a pupil. But Mrs Bartók decided otherwise. Her son should first receive a general education at a grammar school, for she had no intention that he should be an infant prodigy.

There was no grammar school in Nagyszőllős—only an intermediate school—so Béla was sent by his mother to Nágyvárad.[1] There he lived with his aunt, Emma Voit, and after taking the statutory examination was enrolled in the second class of the Grammar School. During the short time he was in Nágyvárad he was taught music by the Music Director of the Cathedral, Ferenc Kersch (1833–1910), who was also a composer. His teaching, however, was superficial and left no lasting influence on his talented pupil.

On 1st May 1892 Béla—now eleven years of age—made his first public appearance as pianist and composer in a charity concert in Nagyszőllős. He played a movement—probably the first—from Beethoven's *Waldstein* Sonata and a com-

[1] Otherwise Grosswardein, and now—the town being Rumanian—Oradea Mare.

position of his own entitled *The River Danube*. The title-page
bore this inscription:

The River Danube,
dedicated to his Mother, Widow Béla Bartók,
composed by Béla Bartók

The young composer had supplied his work with a series of
captions, in order to make clear to everybody what the music
expressed. The performance was very successful, and Béla
was showered with flowers and sweets.

His musical gifts also aroused the enthusiasm of the
Inspector of Schools in Nagyszőllős, whom Mrs Bartók had
to thank for twelve months' leave of absence. She went to
Pressburg (now Bratislava in Czechoslovakia) with Béla,
sent him to the Grammar School in that town and at last
arranged for him to have piano lessons from a really good,
and genuine, musician. This was László Erkel (1844–96), son
of Ferenc Erkel. To his mother's great pleasure, Béla's good
performance at school gained him a scholarship, while books
were made available to him on loan.

In the meanwhile, her leave of absence over, Mrs Bartók
was transferred to Beszterce, which was unwelcome to Béla,
for it meant that here he had no opportunities to pursue his
music studies. It was only acquaintance with a young forester,
named Schönherr, that gave him the chance to take part in
music-making. Schönherr, who not only liked to play the
violin but also played it well, finding no pianist to accompany
him in the town, approached the twelve-year-old boy with
the request that he should play with him. Once a week they
were to be found playing violin and piano sonatas together
at the Bartóks. One evening they performed Beethoven's
Kreutzer Sonata. The impression made on the audience seems
to have been overpowering, for in old age Bartók's sister
Erzsébet recalled this as an unforgettable experience.

Béla dedicated himself to his school-work with great earnestness, and thus—in spite of recurring bouts of ill-health —left the 'Saxon' Grammar School in Beszterce fifth out of forty-five pupils. In April 1894 Mrs Bartók's persistent efforts to exchange her job in Beszterce for one that offered more cultural opportunity were crowned with success. She was given a teaching post in Pressburg, a city with distinguished musical traditions that reached back to the sixteenth century. Ferenc Erkel, the architect of Hungarian national opera, had studied in Pressburg, and it was here that the promise of Franz Liszt was first made apparent.

2 Education in Pressburg

Mrs Bartók took up her new post in the Teachers' College in Széchenyi Street in Pressburg, and Béla went to the Catholic Grammar School. He had to pass examinations in several subjects which were taught here but which had not been in the curriculum in Beszterce, and succeeded in mastering the new material so well in the six weeks available to him that at the end of the school year he passed his examinations in the third class with distinction. In later years Mrs Bartók recalled the efforts that Béla had made to make a good grade in his examinations:

He got up at 6 o'clock and studied before going to school. After meals he went straight to his work, making drawings and doing written exercises—learning, always learning. He didn't touch the piano—which was a great sacrifice; nor did he go to the Danube, although he loved so much to do so. All his time was spent with his schoolwork.

As previously, Bartók's school fees were remitted, and his exertions earned him a scholarship worth 15 Gulden. One of his old schoolfellows, László Aixinger, wrote about Bartók as a student in his *Reminiscences* as follows:

Those of us who were at school at the same time remember him vividly. Every pupil knew him. He had an almost frail physique. The loving care of his mother—widowed early in life—could be appreciated in his clothes, and she made every endeavour to protect him and to keep him away from all that was unpleasant.... What distinguished Bartók from all his schoolfellows, and what struck anyone who met him only once, was the way he looked at one. A mystical, fanatical flame burned in his eyes from time to time—the light of his extraordinary talent and of his genius, as it were.

In the autumn of 1894 Bartók continued his music studies, after having successfully passed his examination, with László Erkel, who was not only a piano-teacher but also a conductor. It is not known how effective Erkel was as a teacher, but Bartók made very rapid progress as a pianist. His introduction to the musical activities of Pressburg was facilitated by Erkel, and soon the name of the talented schoolboy was well known, and not only in his school. With Erkel's help he was now able to obtain free tickets for many concerts and opera performances. In 1894, to take one instance, he heard recitals by the celebrated Hellmesberger Quartet, in which some of the last quartets of Beethoven, as well as some of Haydn's and Schubert's, were given.

In addition to the popular works of Verdi, the Pressburg opera repertory included Bizet's *Carmen*, several works by Lortzing, Nicolai's *Merry Wives of Windsor* and Gounod's *Faust*. In his autobiography Bartók wrote: 'I was able to go to many orchestral concerts and opera performances— though to be sure not of the highest quality. There was also opportunity to practise chamber music, and by the time I was eighteen I had learned the literature of music from Bach to Brahms—though in Wagner no further than *Tannhäuser*— pretty well.'

The chamber music which Bartók 'had the opportunity to practise' was one of the most important features of the musical life of Pressburg. Music was there cultivated in private to a remarkable extent, and Bartók was not long in gaining admittance to the circle of local musical families. In this connection the Inspector of Schools, Roth, who had been responsible for Mrs Bartók's appointment, deserves mention.

By chance, one day, while in the street, he heard Béla's fine piano-playing sounding through an open window, and immediately he sought to make the acquaintance of the young virtuoso. Roth was an excellent cellist and once a week Bartók visited him in his apartment, where they made music together. These musical evenings helped Bartók considerably to extend his knowledge of music.

Dr Frigyes von Dohnányi, who taught physics, mathematics and geography at the Catholic Grammar School, where Bartók was his pupil in these subjects, was also well known among the music-loving intellectuals of Pressburg. Music from a wide repertoire was frequently played at the Dohnányis, the pianist being the doctor's son, Ernő von Dohnányi (1877–1960), who at that time was already a professional and distinguished musician. For a long time Ernő von Dohnányi represented Bartók's ideal of an artist, though being somewhat high-handed in manner he was the complete antithesis to Bartók. Then, as later on and until the end of his life, Bartók found himself facing severe problems of personality and inner difficulties that had to be overcome.

It was, perhaps, at the Dohnányis that Bartók got to know János Batka, who was a lover of music and also wrote about it. Self-educated, Batka had had no formal musical training, but had developed many interests in various directions. He was a close friend of Hans Richter (1843–1916), the world-famous conductor, who was Hungarian in origin, as also of Liszt and Wagner. Batka's selflessness in friendship meant a great deal to the young Bartók. Since he was above the average in musical knowledge—well informed and with some claims to scholarship—he was able to introduce Bartók to interesting and significant works. It is, no doubt, in this association that we find the roots of the great admiration for Liszt that Bartók kept throughout his life. Batka indeed was one of the first Liszt specialists.

In his Pressburg years Bartók found many opportunities to play in public. It was the custom in the Catholic grammar school to assign the organ accompaniment for the Sunday Mass to the most gifted pupil. When the Bartóks came to Pressburg this was done by Ernő von Dohnányi. Later it was undertaken by Bartók. But there were other worthwhile and more interesting opportunities for him to perform in public during his school life. When Hungary reached its millennium in 1896 there was a great celebration in the school. Antal Várady's melodrama, *Rákóczi*, with music by Kornél Ábrányi (1822–1900), was performed, and Bartók played the piano. Programmes of particular festival occasions in the school naturally show signs of what then was generally accepted as 'Hungarian' in flavour. There is an interesting example from 15th March 1898, the Jubilee of the War of Liberation of 1848. The programme was:

1. *Hymnus*, by the school choir
2. Opening address, by Professor Mózes Gaál
3. *Lament not, Lajos Kossuth* [1] by the school choir
4. Festival address, by Géza Bartha (Class VIII)
5. *Bihari's Lament*, violin solo by István Kosutány (Class VII)
6. *Youth and the fifteenth of March*,[2] recited by Ferenc Lajos (Class VIII)
7. *National Song*,[3] recited by Hugo Mayer (Class VII)
8. *Magyars awake*,[3] by the school choir
9. *Forward!*,[3] recited by Gáspár Hanicz (Class VII)

[1] A popular song of the period, as was *Bihari's Lament*.

[2] Inspired by the revolutions in Paris and Vienna earlier in the year, a group of young students, poets and lawyers, among whom Sandor Petöfi, Mór Jókai and Pál Vasvári, were prominent, drew up a manifesto on 15th March 1848, which was the ideological basis of the War of Liberation.

[3] Words by Sándor Petöfi.

10. *Hungarian Folksongs*, by Lajos Bakos (Class VIII)
11. *Hungarian Folksongs*, piano solos by Béla Bartók (Class VII)
12. *Hungary's rebirth* (Mózes Gaál), recited by Gyula Kappel (Class VII)
13. Rákóczy-March, by the school choir and orchestra

This extensive programme gives an idea of the extremely nationalistic tendencies that so strongly affected the people of the towns—at all levels—in the last decade of the nineteenth century. Bartók, of course, did not play proper Hungarian folksongs, but the popular songs of the day which, though of no particular value, were highly favoured at the time. School celebrations were looked after by the Choral and Musical Society of the school, and among the most popular were those concerts given in honour of the Principal's 'Name-day'. After his successful first appearance Bartók took part in all these events. At the 'Name-day' concert of 1897 he played a number of pieces, including Liszt's *Spanish Rhapsody*, and for the same occasion a year later he performed Liszt's arrangement of Wagner's *Tannhäuser* overture.

The Bartóks lived in very modest circumstances, and had to exercise the strictest economy. Béla, therefore, had to try to win scholarships. This he did, for he was a good scholar and also had a good record of conduct. His first award came in 1895 when he gained the Eötvös Prize; the conditions for this he described as follows:

This money prize was to be awarded to a student from a poor family who applied to the Honourable Charity Society and was adjudged by the teaching body to have made the greatest progress in the Hungarian language, provided that Hungarian was not his mother tongue; in the event of there being no such candidate any applicants born in Hungary were eligible.

Despite scholarships the material conditions of the Bartóks

were far from secure. It was only after the most strenuous effort that Mrs Bartók was able to carry out her wishes concerning the education of her children—and especially of Béla. In order to take some of the weight from his mother, whom he loved more than anyone else (her birthday on 16th February was the greatest festival in the family calendar), Béla did some private coaching from the time he was twelve, so that with the money he earned he was at least able to buy music that he needed.

In December 1896 his music-teacher, László Erkel, died, which was a great loss so far as Bartók was concerned. He then went to a teacher named Hyrtl for lessons in piano-playing and counterpoint. By this time he had a brilliant technique on the piano and a developed taste in music, and Hyrtl's teaching was not of the sort to help him make further progress. Hyrtl soon came to the conclusion that there was nothing more that he could do for his pupil, and that there was no point in his continuing to give him lessons, particularly as Bartók was absolutely certain that he would become a pianist. In spite of this aim, however, he cultivated his creative talent with greater intensity. In 1896 he had already produced a violin concerto. In 1897 and 1898 respectively there followed a piano sonata and a piano quartet, and no doubt other works, of which unfortunately there is no record. From this period the only pieces that are now known are some for piano—for instance the three written in 1897 and dedicated to Gabriella Lator. (Gabriella was a childhood friend of Bartók in Nagyszőllős, and the friendship continued into later years.) There is also known a *Scherzo* in B minor, which has many resemblances to the youthful works of Brahms.

It would naturally be wrong to expect to find characteristic Bartók traits in these early works. The same may be said of the *Three Songs* of 1898, of which the first is contained in facsimile in Vol. I of Bartók's letters. This is a setting of

Heine's poem *Im wunderschönen Monat Mai* (in German). Melody and harmony are somewhat monotonous and conventional, while there are even errors of declamation to be found. However, in spite of this, musical circles in Pressburg were convinced by these songs that Bartók would become a great and famous artist—like Ernő von Dohnányi—and soon he had further opportunities for developing his talents. Dohnányi, who had already completed his final examinations, usually spent the summer holidays at home. He spoke a good deal about István Thomán, the piano-teacher with whom he studied in Budapest. Thomán had been a pupil of Liszt, and this was decisive for Bartók, who resolved to continue his musical education at the Academy in Budapest.

But before this could be put into effect Bartók travelled to Vienna on 8th December 1898, to sit for an examination at the Conservatorium. He took a number of compositions with him, and he played his piano sonata. The judgment of the Viennese professors was very favourable. His extraordinary talent was confirmed and, although he was a Hungarian, they wanted him to enter the institution at once, without fee and with other offers of help. But Bartók stood by his resolution to study in Budapest.

In January 1899 mother and son went to Budapest, and on Dohnányi's advice Bartók presented himself to Professor Thomán. He played fugues by Bach, Beethoven's *Appassionata* Sonata, and the Paganini-Liszt Study in A Minor. Thomán was so delighted with Bartók's piano-playing that he assured Mrs Bartók that her son could be accepted as a student of the Academy in the autumn without examination. At Thomán's suggestion Bartók also saw Hans Koessler (1853–1926), professor of composition, to whom he showed —as first choice from his stock of works so far completed— his piano quartet. Koessler's opinion was also very favourable. Several weeks after the journey to Budapest, when it could have been expected that Thomán hardly remembered the young man's name, Bartók had a letter in which Thomán invited him to spend a day in Budapest. The reason for this was that Hans Richter was to conduct Beethoven's Ninth Symphony with the Philharmonic Orchestra. Bartók accepted the invitation with pleasure, and on 27th March 1899 he heard the performance. At that time this great work was only seldom played in the Hungarian capital.

After this journey Bartók was taken seriously ill. The doctor forbade him to play the piano and limited his school work to one or two hours a day. Nevertheless, he passed his final examination with a 'good' grade. When he had got over his illness he went with his mother to convalesce at Eberhard in Kärnten, where he fully recovered.

3 The Academy of Music in Budapest

Endowed with a knowledge of the most important works in the European musical repertory, a talent capable of development, and determination, Bartók began his studies at the Academy of Music in Budapest in 1899. At this time music in the Hungarian capital was in a very flourishing condition, with opera as the focal point of interest. The period of 1888–1891, in which it was directed by Gustav Mahler (1860–1911), had been one of brilliance and the after-effects were still to be felt. Unfortunately the second great musical institution, the Philharmonic Orchestra, showed up unfavourably in comparison. The reason for this was not so much the players—for the most part recruited from among the members of the opera orchestra—as the conductors, whose accomplishments were no more than average. Because guest conductors from abroad achieved nothing outstanding (a newspaper observed that conductors of similar ability were also to be found in Hungary) a stronger light fell on the solo performers. Among these Eugen d'Albert—for his thrilling Beethoven interpretations—and Jan Kubelík—a violin virtuoso who reminded some of Paganini—aroused the greatest enthusiasm.

There were some outstanding personalities at the Academy of Music when Bartók began his studies there. Ferenc Erkel's (1810–93) successor as director was Ödön Mihalovich (1842–1929). Mihalovich was a fine teacher and an experienced composer who, among other works, had written an opera based on Wagner's outline libretto for *Wieland the Smith*. He recognized Bartók's talent at the outset and energetically sought to foster it (as he did, a little later, with Kodály's) by every means at his disposal. During Mihalovich's term of office the Academy was given a new building, which became a firm base for the ever-increasing musical life of Hungary.

As successor to Robert Volkmann (1815–83) the composition department was looked after by Hans Koessler (1853–1926), a cousin of Max Reger. Although the Academy was an offshoot of the German school—necessarily, since both Volkmann and Koessler were of German extraction—Koessler, because of his great ability, helped a whole generation of Hungarian composers, among whom were Bartók, Kodály and Leó Weiner (1885–1960), to develop. The best-known piano-teacher was Thomán, who has already been mentioned. Like Mihalovich he immediately recognized Bartók's talent and was at pains to foster it. What Thomán showed over and above his artistic and pedagogic competence was the will to establish personal contact with his pupils. More than once Bartók had occasion to be grateful to him for his friendly concern. On 24th September 1899, shortly after he had begun his studies, he wrote to his mother:

Professor Thomán was interesting today. At 10.45, after the lesson, he called me to him and asked why I was wearing shoes, because early today it was so chilly. He thought, in fact, that I must have been there as early as 9 o'clock. But I said that Mr Szabó had let me off his lesson . . . I said I was grateful for his concern, however, which really was very nice of him.

On 21st January 1900 he sent more details home:

Mr Thomán again did all sorts of things for me. He said that I should buy the Schubert Impromptu in the Liszt edition, but I told him that it wasn't possible this month because I had no money. So he bought it for me 'as a souvenir'. Then I was able to go to the [Emil von] Sauer concert free through his good offices, and to sell the ticket I had already bought. After that he gave me a copy of the *Valkyrie*. He also spoke with the Director about the scholarship.

When Bartók came to Thomán, according to what he himself said, he had a relatively good technique. This statement means a good deal, taking into consideration that for the whole of his life he was extremely moderate in judgment—especially concerning himself. For the rest, he also said he was a 'real savage' when he played the piano—brutal, hard and rough. Thomán wanted to eliminate such unevenness and hardness and to induce him to cultivate a more artistic manner. He taught him the flexibility and artistic perception belonging to the modern technique which he himself had learnt from Liszt. Thomán never wished to dam the personality of his pupil, nor to influence his ideas or his ideals. He belonged to that rare body of teachers who do not suppress the individuality of those they teach but deem it their duty to encourage and develop it.

It was his chief concern, therefore, that the pupil should in the first place play any piece being studied with precision and reliability. When this was achieved he made it his duty to bring out personal qualities of artistry so that the pupil's individuality and personality could appear. He did not, however, consider himself infallible, but on the contrary suggested to students that they should listen to other pianists. He often had celebrated artists as his guests, so that his protégés were able to hear them and to study their performance at close quarters. Thomán also considered it of supreme importance that his pupils should be able to prove their skills in public. He took pains to see that they never went on to the concert platform unprepared. His motto was: 'The art of performance is not only a matter of knowing, but also of being able to show that one knows.'

At the beginning of October 1899 Mrs Bartók had a letter

from her son's landlady to say that he was very ill. She went to Budapest immediately and called in a well-known doctor, who advised that Béla should give up his career as a pianist. Another doctor—tuberculosis was hinted at—recommended him to return home in order to get well there. Bartók went back to Budapest in December, at first taking rooms on the Buda side of the Danube, where the air was better and more healthy than in Pest. His aunt, Irma Voit, looked after his housekeeping. However, he very soon went back to Pest, to be nearer to the Academy, and threw himself into his work with ardour so that he could make up for lost time. In 1899–1900 he studied, among others, the following works: fourteen items from *The Well-Tempered Clavier*, and the *Italian Concerto*, by Bach; the A flat major Sonata (Op. 26) and the C minor Concerto of Beethoven; Schumann's *Fantasiestücke*; and Chopin's Preludes.

Koessler's classes in composition were held twice a week, and every student who had shown good progress (Bartók was among them) was allowed to play Liszt's piano, made by the American firm of Chickering. Each student played his composition while the others stood around the piano, encouraged by Koessler to criticize the piece being played. Bartók's remarkable gifts as a pianist made everyone take notice of him during the first lessons, whereas as a composer he had difficulties to cope with from the start. Koessler was certainly a good teacher but, belonging to the older generation, he was relatively hostile to Bartók's compositions.

On 5th January 1900 Béla wrote to his mother:

Yesterday I took my quintet; but Mr Koessler said that the whole thing was not good, and that I might like to begin something else— in *Lied* form. What it was that was not good I do not know, since he spoke only in general terms—that one must choose better themes, etc. That means that not a single theme is any good. But if these were valueless I do not know if I could write any better in,

21

for example, a year. Above all, why didn't he tell me last January that my pieces were no good? In my opinion this quintet is in every way better than last year's quartet.

Koessler's antipathy to Bartók's style of composition grew stronger and stronger, although he was unable to produce any plausible justification for it. In the autumn of 1902 Bartók wrote to his mother as follows:

I took the slow movement to Koessler today. He said: 'In an Adagio there must be love; but in this movement there is no sign of love. This is a mistake. But it is one of the disadvantages of modern composers that they can't produce Adagios.' For this reason composers keep out of his way as far as possible. But he can't expect from me what one can't wish for from others. I would like, therefore, to continue it (i.e. the Symphony). If I don't get any better ideas, this movement can remain, although it cannot be said to have been a success—it is well known that Koessler is very severe in his criticism of Adagios. He keeps on saying: 'A man must have had some experience to be able to write an Adagio.' (What?! Probably love and what belongs to it—disappointments, raptures, pain, etc.) Well, I don't believe that experience has any influence on the quality of composition. I have already had various experiences. I also have talent (people say so, at least), so, according to the given rule, I ought to be able to write good Adagios. What's more, he doesn't consider Dohnányi's Adagios above criticism. (Nor do I!)

Since Bartók continued to believe that the only worthwhile career was that of a pianist, Koessler's carping did not irritate him overmuch; on the other hand he strove to improve his piano technique by listening to famous players. He was often to be seen at concerts, where he heard d'Albert, Sauer, Teresa Carreño [1] and Dohnányi.

On 18th May he made his first appearance before the Buda-

---

[1] Venezuelan pianist (1853–1917), educated in New York. Eugen d'Albert was one of her husbands.

pest public, as accompanist to a celebrated artist. He reported to his mother as follows:

I was delighted finally to be able to play with a real artist, and also to make the acquaintance of a lovable man. It began this way. I played with [Adolf] Schiffer, who had spoken to [Dávid] Popper about me, asking if I couldn't accompany him this time. Popper said he had no objections, so I went to him on Sunday. Then he told me that I was a good sight-reader, and finally thanked me five times for coming to him. . . . And this evening I called for him, and then we went to the Park Club.

Bartók had no kind of payment for his concert, although Popper had solemnly sworn that he would take care of that. Living as he did in very modest circumstances, Bartók badly needed the money. In the postscript to his letter of 21st January 1900 to his mother we read: 'At the moment I have eight (repeat, eight) Kreuzer, but tomorrow morning I get the Gulden for my Sauer ticket. A week ago I was in the same kind of predicament.'

Despite these circumstances, however, he passed the second year examinations of the Academy with outstanding success. During the summer holidays he went with his mother to Heberstein (Steiermark). The first part of the holidays went by uneventfully but near the end, on 17th August, he felt unwell, and the doctor diagnosed inflammation of the lungs. Because of this he was unable to undertake the return journey until 15th September. At home his condition worsened and gave rise to considerable anxiety. The doctor advised Mrs Bartók to take Béla to Meran. After a good deal of trouble she took six months' leave, so that they could stay in Meran until 1st April 1901. Bartók recovered, and his zest for life also returned when the doctor told him in January that he might take up piano-playing again. In an article—'Bartók, the man' —Kodály wrote: 'After his stay in Meran . . . he came back so stout that he could have been described as stocky.'

During his studies Bartók took every opportunity to get to know Wagner's late works better—*The Ring*, *The Master-singers* and *Tristan*. He wrote to his mother: 'Last Monday I studied the score of *The Rhinegold* (a bequest from Liszt) in one of the rooms in the Academy. It is very interesting; I have found much (that I have never noticed before) that is greatly instructive.'

Later he told her: 'Now I am studying *The Valkyrie*; this is much more beautiful than *The Rhinegold*.' Nevertheless he did not neglect the piano; in fact he made progress. In the academic year 1901–2 he busied himself among other works with the following: eight of Chopin's Preludes; two Preludes and Fugues from Bach's 'Forty-eight'; the Diabelli Variations of Beethoven; Brahms's Handel-Variations; and various works by Liszt, including the B minor Sonata.

The longer he stayed in Budapest, the larger and more varied his circle of acquaintances grew. Among others, he came to know the Arányi family, who were closely related to Joseph Joachim—the world-famous violinist who was of Hungarian origin. Both the Arányi daughters were also pre-paring themselves for the career of violin virtuoso. The elder, Adila, was a pupil of her great-uncle Joseph; the younger, Jelly, who began her studies somewhat later, became, like her sister, a celebrated player. In the autumn of 1900 Bartók had this to say of the Arányis in one of his letters:

One day this week it happened that the Arányis kindly invited me to visit them on Sunday afternoon, because they were to have a small gathering of young musicians there. Kerpely (he is now the best cellist in the Academy) was to be there, and Sabathiel, a 'violin virtuoso' (who got his diploma last year)—and so on. I do not know whether I shall go. On the one hand I am nervous of this 'society'; on the other, up to now my Sunday afternoons—which I have spent alone—have been pretty awful, and this isn't the kind of group one would find at a reception or at a soirée.

Third, the Arányi family is very interesting; first because of their close relationship with Joachim (the daughters' paternal grandmother was Joachim's sister); second, because there is no word of German spoken since no single member of the family knows any. (Instead of German they know French.)

Bartók was often a guest of the family of Felicitás Fábián. This girl—a fellow student—studied not only the piano but also composition, which was then rare for a woman. Koessler was very well pleased with her progress in this direction—as Bartók reported to his mother in a letter of 16th June 1900.

Becoming acquainted with Mrs Henrik Gruber was significant for Bartók in another way. She was a sister of Pál Sándor, a Member of Parliament who played an important role in Hungarian economic life. Musically she was extraordinarily well educated, even to the extent of being an active composer. She was very young when she married a rich Budapest merchant, Henrik Gruber, who made it possible for her to maintain a musical salon. Everyone who was anybody in music went there. Koessler, a good friend of her father's, and Mihalovich, Viktor Herzfeld, Ernő von Dohnányi and many others were often Mrs Gruber's guests. But young musicians of talent were welcomed too, and they were able to meet with important personalities in the world of music. Mrs Gruber not only entertained young artists—who were for the most part unaccustomed to so splendid an environment—but also helped them to get to know the most modern music, which was not readily accessible. She learned from Koessler, or maybe somewhat earlier from Mihalovich, of the exceptional talent of Béla Bartók. She invited him to her house and he was much talked about on account of his marvellous score-reading. In the autumn of 1902 he wrote to his mother, saying how he had been congratulated on his playing of Dohnányi's Symphony (Op. 9) from the score:

Mrs Gruber was delighted not only with the work, but also with my playing of it. So was everyone else... The whole work lasts an hour. The opinion of the amateurs was that the public would enjoy the second movement, and perhaps also the third; but not the first and fourth, for these are too complicated. It's a pity! Because I liked it all. I got home finally at half-past eight. Then I tried the Symphony over again, and was amazed to find that already I knew the first three movements by heart.

Bartók used also to play from full score in later years and became more and more accomplished in this art. When he was a professor he would play from manuscript scores at the composition examinations, when the students concerned declined to do so.

As has already been mentioned, Bartók was not only released from the obligation of paying for his course at the Academy, but also enjoyed the goodwill and readiness to help of his professors. He was, therefore, in receipt of different grants, for which Mihalovich in the first place was responsible. He wrote the following sentence privately after he had had an application from Bartók (probably in 1903): 'He is one of the most outstanding [students], conspicuous by reason of his talent, tireless zeal, and exemplary behaviour, and he justifies the highest hopes.' Whoever met Bartók must have recognized him as one with a sense of vocation. He was an extremely serious man, who could relax only in an intimate circle of family or friends. Then he was a marvellous companion, sparkling with ideas and humour. So far as strangers were concerned, however, he maintained a certain reserve. His way of life was fundamentally different from that of the other artists, for he played no games, did not drink and kept away from cafés. At that time a great part of the public and cultural business of Budapest was conducted in cafés, where the intellectuals found their real home. But Bartók avoided this kind of 'artistic' life.

The time had now arrived for him to do his military service as a one-year volunteer. Fortunately, however, his application for release was granted and he could continue his studies without impediment. He had lost a whole year of his education through illness, but after his recovery had committed himself to his work with enormous energy to make up for lost time. In this he had been successful. On 21st October 1901, on the night before the celebration of Liszt's birthday, he gave a performance of the B minor Sonata at a public memorial concert in the Academy. The critics present, without exception, were full of praise and appreciation.

During his free time Bartók enjoyed the beautiful environs of Budapest. All his life he felt himself to be in close communion with nature. He loved long walks, during which he would live with his own thoughts or talk with a friend. Two concepts completely integrated—one of the freedom of nature, the other of human freedom—so affected Bartók that they changed his whole personality. Love of his native countryside was a most important ingredient of his patriotism.

One who was as alert as Bartók naturally found as much interest as he wanted in the goings-on of the artistic world, but he also concerned himself with more remote spheres of knowledge. From his love of nature sprang an inclination towards natural history, but he also expended much energy on learning foreign languages. He had a collector's passion too, and his range of interest in this respect extended from works on folk-art to insects and forms of exotic expression. It is notable that he did not stop at merely collecting objects but arranged everything in systematic order.

The next concert in which he was involved took place in the Leopoldstadt Casino on 14th December 1901. Since this event was open to the press, and was a great social event, a large number of complimentary notices appeared, the general tenor of which was that Thomán's young pupil had a great future ahead of him as a pianist. This time there was a fee of 100 Gulden—actually Bartók's first—which he gave his mother as a Christmas present.

A musical event of this time that especially excited him was the performance of Richard Strauss's symphonic poem *Also sprach Zarathustra* on 12th February 1902. In his autobiography he wrote:

The work, dismissed by most of the musicians of Budapest, filled me with the greatest enthusiasm. At last I found a point of view which offered something new. I threw myself into the study of Strauss's scores and began to compose again. There was something else that was significant and decisive so far as my development was concerned. At that time there arose a familiar chauvinistic tendency which also made itself felt in the field of the arts. It was worth while creating something specifically Hungarian in music.

What he then felt to be Hungarian he showed in his first published work of 1902—the set of *Four Songs*.

The texts of the songs were by Lajos Pósa, and they were certainly under the influence of this chauvinistic tendency. The melodic style of the song-cycle is also influenced by the same tendency which, a few years later, Bartók opposed with all power and energy. Melodically these works differed hardly at all from those of the composers of the day who counted as 'Hungarian'; but characteristic traits evident in later Bartók are noticeable in the harmony. For example, in one place in the second song (from bar 17) the accompaniment has this shape:

Similar pedal points are not to be found anywhere in the works of Bartók's contemporaries. A few bars later the following progression is to be found:

This sudden modulation, adopted maybe from Liszt, is also very typical of the later Bartók. For the six-four chord used in this manner there are parallels only in Debussy, whose music, however, was not known to Bartók at that time. The most interesting and best of the songs is the third, which begins with a chord without the third:

This by itself brought something new to Hungarian music. Also in this song there is the following passage:

ró - zsa - szál

In the first and fifth bars a descending figure is to be found, which often occurs in a similar way in Bartók's later music. The whole of the third song strongly reminds one of the volume of *Eight Hungarian Folksongs* of 1917.

Unfortunately the students of the Academy had great difficulty in getting to know contemporary orchestral works, since these were seldom performed by the Philharmonic Society. They had to go to the morning and afternoon concerts given at the St Luke's Bath (a thermal bath on the right bank of the Danube) by the Wieschendorf Orchestra.

It is not at all surprising that Bartók's enthusiasm for 'ultra-modern' music was disapproved of by professors of the older generation. Those who were of German extraction, or at least under the influence of German music, could hardly appreciate that it was Bartók's aim in life to produce a 'specifically Hungarian' kind of music. Koessler, particularly, closed his mind to everything modern with great determination. Mihalovich also was hostile, although in the case of Bartók (whose talent he appreciated at first sight) he tried to put his own opinions into the background.

What everybody could appreciate, and about which there could be no doubt, was Bartók's pianistic talent. On this all his professors were agreed. So he enjoyed the special privilege of being able to play at professional gatherings which were from time to time organized so that new and unknown works by Hungarian and foreign composers could be heard by a select audience. On one of these occasions Jenő von Hubay played the violin in a work by Bartók and was accompanied by the composer.

In December of this year Bartók played Strauss's *Ein Heldenleben* at Mrs Gruber's house, and afterwards had to repeat this remarkable performance for the benefit of the teaching body of the Academy. This time he played this difficult work from memory, which caused more of a sensation. Professor Viktor Herzfeld, who soon afterwards returned to Vienna, was there. He was more than generous in his praise of Bartók, who before long received an invitation to go to Vienna on 26th January 1903 to play the Strauss work yet again—this time for the Society of Musicians. The performance left a strong impression, and people in Vienna remembered it for years.

On 6th February 1903 Bartók wrote to his mother:

I played a new work of my own with which I 'achieved much success'. . . . It is a sonata movement for left hand only, which sounds however as if I played it with three hands.

Leopold Godowsky enjoyed these pieces, and remarked that the one for left hand had good ideas. He also criticized something in it, and I will use his suggestion, since in so far as this is concerned it will make for improvement. Finally he said 'Out of that something great will emerge'.

The *Study for left hand*, mentioned by Bartók in this letter, was generally acclaimed, doubtless because of the absolute mastery of his own performance. In another letter he reported that Koessler, having been shown the work, had nothing to say against it. It is strongly influenced by Liszt and Brahms and makes great demands on the technical resources of the performer. On Easter Monday, 13th April 1903, Bartók gave his first independent recital in his birthplace, Nagyszentmiklós. As well as works by Chopin and Liszt the programme contained two of his own compositions—the *Study for left hand* and the *Fantasia.*

Meanwhile the time of the final examinations drew near, but because of his brilliant efforts both as pianist and composer Bartók was excused from them. For the sake of form he only took part in the concert arranged by the Academy students, playing Liszt's *Spanish Rhapsody.* On 25th May 1903 he wrote to his mother: 'To the great surprise of my colleagues I shall not take my examinations, since the general opinion is that this is superfluous.'

In the course of his last student years Bartók studied, among others, these works: Brahms's F minor Sonata and Paganini Variations; Schumann's F sharp minor Sonata; Bach's C minor Partita; and Beethoven's Sonata in C minor, Op. 111. Already at the beginning of the year he had announced to his mother his intention of undertaking further study with Dohnányi during the summer. About this he wrote: 'He [Dohnányi] will teach me, but only so long as I say nothing to anyone about it; for he will have no other pupil. This is all right so far as I am concerned . . . It is most likely that the "tuition" will be given in Gmunden in the summer.' Dohnányi and his wife received Bartók in a kindly spirit, as he testified in a letter on 23rd August: 'The Dohnányis are very friendly to me. On Saturday I had lunch with them. The old people are here and also the professor's sister-in-law. During the afternoon he took me on an excursion to Trautmannsdorf, in which Koessler took part too.'

Bartók felt altogether in such good form at Gmunden that he worked particularly hard, most of all at composition. He gave the final shape to his Sonata—especially the slow movement—which he wanted to submit for the Rubinstein Competition in Paris. He also finished the orchestration of his *Kossuth* Symphony. Dohnányi had nothing to say about this work at first, but later 'he raised a thousand and one objections over the most insignificant things'. It seems that he felt that Bartók was an iconoclast and that he recognized the vast difference between his and Bartók's emotional and idealistic spheres of interest. They often liked to engage in political discussions, and even at the beginning of his stay in Gmunden Bartók remarked to his mother: 'We talk with Dohnányi a great deal—about the political situation. It is quite natural that he does not support the national demands, but we cannot convince each other.' Because his mother assumed from this that he had fallen out with Dohnányi, he answered her four weeks later: 'You are wrong about Dohnányi. I regard him highly as man and artist. As an artist he is much too severe concerning his colleagues, but this is no great fault. Much greater and unforgivable is his lack of patriotism. This makes it unlikely that a "closer relationship" will ever develop between us.' This regular exchange of opinions strengthened Bartók's patriotic sentiments, as the following lines, also written during his Gmunden visit, on 8th September, prove:

Everyone, on reaching maturity, must decide for what ideal he will fight, so that all his work, all his actions, can be directed to that end. For my part I will devote every part of my life, always and in every way, to one good: the good of the Hungarian nation and of the Hungarian fatherland.

Bartók remained true to this vow to the end of his life.

As well as those works that have been mentioned, he wrote the *Scherzo* which was later included among the *Four Piano Pieces* and dedicated it to Dohnányi. In writing to his friend Lajos Dietl he indicated that the summer visit to Gmunden was anything but a period of rest:

I am scarcely able to enjoy the beautiful surroundings, for the writing out and correction of my compositions involve so much labour. It is unbelievable how much work there is in preparing a score so that parts may be copied. At the moment I have three such scores to attend to with due care: two copies of 'Kossuth' and an orchestral Scherzo, for which—since it is down for a concert in October—I am responsible to the Academy.

Soon after he had sent this letter Bartók went to Berlin, where he gave a piano recital in the Saal Bechstein on 14th December. After Berlin he went again to Vienna to play Beethoven's *Emperor* Concerto with great success at a performance organized by the Concert Society and conducted by Ernst von Schuch from Dresden.

In his letters from Berlin Bartók could not say often enough how pleased he felt to be there. The reason for this, doubtless, was that here he was able to meet the most distinguished personalities in the field of music, and that they all appreciated his gifts. He made the acquaintance of Busoni, who had already heard of him from Hans Richter. Unfortunately he was unable to meet Strauss, since Godowsky—on whom Bartók relied in this instance—was not in a position to arrange an introduction.

Bartók wrote about his visit to Berlin on 29th October 1903:

Getting to know people goes on like an avalanche. Up to now six or eight of the introductions have only resulted in two visits . . . Yesterday evening the virtuoso violinist Kreisler and his wife—as well as other people—were at Godowsky's. (On Monday he played with the Philharmonic.) I played 'Kossuth', Dohnányi's Passacaglia, my Scherzo and the Study for left hand, and there was much applause. (Everyone is much impressed beforehand by the Manchester performance.)

The final sentence means that it was already settled that the *Kossuth* Symphony—through the good offices of Richter—was to be played in Manchester.

For the most part Bartók derived only moral benefits from his Berlin visit. He had no talent for making use of new acquaintances for the furthering of his future prospects. In this respect he was always somewhat awkward and never given either to flattery or boasting. Very likely he believed that his talent—recognized by everybody who met him and of which, despite his almost excessive modesty, he was always aware himself—would be enough to set him safely on the road to success. Unfortunately this was not so. He lived in a world where even the greatest talent had to struggle for recognition, and for this the necessary qualities, so far as he was concerned, were lacking. This is why his life was, in a material sense, unsuccessful, and why his works did not enjoy the wider recognition that they deserved.

4 The *Kossuth* Symphony

On 13th January 1904 István Kerner conducted the first performance of the *Kossuth* Symphony in the great hall of the Budapest Redoute. The newspaper critics reflected a great variety of contrasted opinions. The work, however, did create an extraordinary sensation; in many reviews it was generously noticed and even enthusiastically praised. On 14th January the *Pesti Napló* said:

. . . Bartók's talents triumphed today, and with his first work he put himself at once in the company of Ernő von Dohnányi, who up to now, among the new school of Hungarian composers, had led the field with his splendid Symphony in D minor.

. . . In spite of all its elaboration the public gave the work a really enthusiastic reception, which made a tremendous impression. After the first burst of applause for István Kerner, the young composer was called for. He had a tremendous ovation—of a rare intensity —and was recalled to the platform ten times. From today, together with Dohnányi, who is a few years older, he joins the company of the most significant masters of Hungarian music.

[Tivadar Landor.]

The same issue of the *Pesti Napló* contained the following as a news item:

In connection with today's performance of the *Kossuth* Symphony we must mention a painful scandal that almost made the performance of this important work impossible. When the rehearsal of the symphony was taking place several members of the Philharmonic Society created a noisy scene, thus interrupting the study of a work written to honour Kossuth and the Hungarian War of Liberation. We know that Kossuth's name is unpleasant to Austrian ears, but we had never thought it possible that any Austrian living on Hungarian soil could have dared to make such a demonstration.

. . . When the orchestra reached the parodied 'Emperor's Hymn' some members of the Philharmonic stopped playing, loudly protesting that they would neither play this part of the work, nor suffer anyone else to play it, since it was not permissible to play the Hymn thus distorted. All explanations and attempts at persuasion were in vain. The Austrian musicians—living on Hungarian bread—went on complaining. Thus began a stormy scene which was ended by Professor Kerner putting down his baton and leaving the rehearsal room. The Philharmonic players, shocked, asked to go on working at the Symphony until he made up his mind what to do.

Under these circumstances it is of interest to report that five members of the orchestra, all players of important instruments, absented themselves from the Philharmonic Concert today. They sent medical certificates, and their absence all but made the performance of the *Kossuth* Symphony impossible.

I quote this to indicate the attempts made to place political obstacles in the way of a truly patriotic work.

On 14th January 1904 the performance was reported with especial affection by the *Pester Lloyd*, the notice ending:

Although there are youthful extravagances, and a number of places marked by obscurity or palpable derivations, Bartók's talent, as shown in the 'Kossuth' Symphony, is considerable. He has astonishing technical competence, an unusual sense of colour, and a powerful—indeed fiery—temperament. Today he has awakened the highest expectations and achieved a well-deserved success. The young composer was loudly recalled to the platform some dozen times. There was no lack of bouquets. . . .

The symphony remained unpublished until 1963. The following are the principal themes, given here with Bartók's own captions:

Bartók

'1. 'Kossuth'.

2. 'What sorrow weighs on your soul, dear husband?'
(Kossuth's wife)

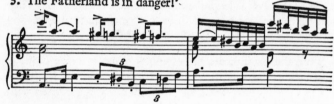

3. 'The Fatherland is in danger!'

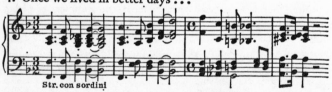

4. 'Once we lived in better days ...'

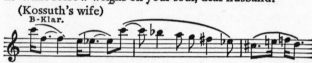

5. 'But our plight grew worse'

6. 'To battle!'

7. 'Come forth, ye Magyar heroes of true valour'

8. ... (Theme of the Austrian army slowly approaching)

9. 'All is over'

It may be assumed that the first performance of the *Kossuth* Symphony was far from faultless. Although Kerner was a good conductor the conditions described in the *Pesti Napló* made a perfect interpretation of a modern work impossible. Nevertheless the work was generally praised, and for this the political climate could have been responsible. Hatred of the House of Hapsburg at the beginning of the century was so great in Hungary that it united the most diverse political views and parties.

The performance of the *Kossuth* Symphony, under Richter, in Manchester, was probably very much better than that in Budapest. Bartók was there and played the piano during the

39

same concert. There are interesting comments about the symphony (particularly its first English performance) by John Foulds:

About the year 1903 Béla Bartók ... brought to his compatriot and mentor Hans Richter, a work for orchestra which he had written under the impetus received from Richard Strauss. The latter's *Zarathustra* had made a profound impression upon Bartók whose musical education had previously been conducted on strictly classical lines. The exhilarating effect of this work, allied to his love of the Fatherland, resulted in a tone-poem having the national hero *Kossuth* as its central figure. It contained, I remember, a *fugato* upon Haydn's quartet-tune which had been adopted by Austria as a national anthem.[1] As youths together we discussed the work, practically his first for large orchestra (he was a modest, keen fellow, his English sparse, my German even more so), and his dissatisfaction with the *fugato* in question prompted the suggestion that a little research would probably have discovered a genuine Hungarian folk-tune which might more happily have rounded off the episode.[2]

During Bartók's visit to England his 'examination piece', which had been performed at the Diploma Concert of the Academy in Budapest, was also given a hearing. This *Scherzo for Orchestra* subsequently had a good press in Hungary.

After his English visit Bartók went to Berlin, where he remained from the middle of March until the end of April. Then he went to Pressburg for two days and finally to Gerlice-Puszta (in Gömör County). In the peace and quiet of this small country town he worked intensively on his compositions—probably on the Piano Quartet and the Rhapsody

---

[1] The 'Emperor's Hymn', of course, came first, its melody subsequently being used by Haydn in the *Emperor* Quartet.

[2] *Music Today* (London, 1934), p. 254. The account of the performance in *The Manchester Guardian* of 19th February 1904 is reprinted in Appendix E (p. 208).

for Piano and Orchestra (Op. 1). Dedicated to Mrs Gruber
('To Emma'), this work is dated November 1904.

In spite of the success which Bartók had achieved, his
material circumstances grew worse and worse. Nor were the
grants which he regularly received sufficient to enable him to
work and to compose in tranquillity. He spent June 1904 in
Vésztő (Békés County) with his sister, who had married a
property inspector named Emil von Oláh Tóth. Here he
completed his Rhapsody, which was entirely influenced by
the Hungarian Rhapsodies of Liszt. Common to the two
composers is the division into two sections—the first slow
and sustained, the second quick and dance-like.

The principal themes of both sections have a gipsy quality,
and so are not far distant from the folk-music of Hungary.
The tonality is based on the major and minor scales and there
is nothing out-of-the-way in the harmony. Nevertheless the
whole work is so lively and full of energy that it deserves
frequent concert performance. An idea of the character of the
work may be gained from a closer consideration of the
principal themes.

After two bars of cadenza-like introduction the first theme
appears:

Together with an ancillary motiv this is worked out in a kind
of sonata movement. The brass instruments announce a new
theme:

After this the opening subject reappears in altered form and a coda leads to the second section. The principal theme of the second section is related to the second theme of the first:

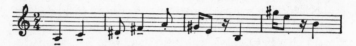

It was in Vésztő that Bartók, for the first time in his life, came across true Hungarian folk-music, in the songs of the peasantry. This encounter, although not yet decisive for his later work, did in fact lay its foundations. During the next year he was already beginning systematically to collect folk-songs.

First, however, he had to prepare himself for the fifth Rubinstein Competition, which was to take place in Paris. The terms of the competition required the performance of the following works: the second and third movement of Rubinstein's G major Piano Concerto, a four-part fugue by Bach, one of the last Sonatas of Beethoven, three works by Schumann, one or two by Chopin and, finally, a Study by Liszt. Pianists and composers were eligible to take part in this competition, established in honour of the celebrated Russian musician, which took place every five years in a different European capital. Bartók was practically certain that he would gain a prize for composition. He had faith in his ability and he anticipated not only moral but also material success. That he was not awarded the first prize, therefore, made his disappointment greater. He was, in fact, given no award by the jury, nor any other kind of recognition.

Leopold Auer (1845–1930), President of the Jury, who as a virtuoso violinist was active in St Petersburg, said of Bartók's composition: 'Yes, this is the new school—but we're a bit too old for this sort of thing!' Camille Chevillard (1859–1923) found it interesting, and Gustav Hollaender,

Director of the Stern Academy in Berlin, wanted to play Bartók's Violin Sonata, one of the works submitted for the composition prize. But the jury would have none of it.

On 15th August, immediately after the depressing result of the competition was announced, Bartók remarked, with some satisfaction, that he was glad at least to have seen a new city —Paris—and to have made new acquaintances. He went on:

I'm sorry to tell you that I had no success in the Competition. It is neither extraordinary nor disturbing that I won nothing in the piano class. But what happened in respect of the chief award— that is, the non-chief award—for composition is shocking. . . .

What is most scandalous is that the jury did not see how much better my works were [than those of the other competitors].

The pieces were performed quite reasonably well. That the judges did not appreciate this is an even greater scandal.

And what a great scurry there was! I almost had to withdraw. I was told that the *Concertstück* [i.e. the Rhapsody for Piano and Orchestra] had mistakes in the parts; it was very difficult; there was only a little time available for rehearsal; the work, therefore, couldn't be performed. I corrected the parts . . . and after much coming and going the work was put on quite respectably.

The other four composers produced entirely worthless things. If a quite tolerable composer had taken the prize from me I wouldn't have said a word. But that these beasts should have declared my things unworthy of the prize, that is only a sign of an unheard-of stupidity. . . .

Paris is marvellous, but I only now have time really to enjoy it, for up to now the pace has been too much.

On the same day Bartók wrote to the pianist Irmy Jurkovics, a companion of his childhood. Among other things in a long letter he said:

The English pianist Backhaus [1] won the piano prize, and he played

[1] Backhaus was, of course, German. At this time, however, he was resident in Manchester, where he was on the professorial staff of the Royal Manchester College of Music.

really beautifully. I'm mad! Because so much superfluous labour went into the competition . . . and because I had not reckoned on this result. . . . One thing comforts me, that at least I came to Paris, this divine, ungodly city. I cannot describe the beautiful things there are here—the focal point of the world. They must be seen. What great art has gone into the building of Paris! What, in comparison, are Vienna, or Berlin! (I still expect much from Budapest, apart from the old treasures of art which can never be replaced.)

The Paris visit had also its positive side, for it extended quite considerably his mental horizons. He stayed in a *pension*, where he had the opportunity to meet representatives of the most diverse nations: American, English, German, French, South American, Turkish, etc. We know from his letter that his great disappointment severely depressed him, but that none the less he was responsive to new experiences and impressions. For instance, he wrote to Irmy Jurkovics: 'I walked in the Jardin des plantes beneath cedars of Lebanon, and in the Boulevard des Italiens I bought *Pesti Hirlap* and *A Nap*[1] (genuine exotic items!).' Although he was a lifelong patriot he observed in the same letter:

Bach, Beethoven, Schubert and Wagner have written so much music of character that in relation to it all French, Italian and Slav music taken together amounts to very little. Liszt is somewhere near greatness, but he seldom composes Hungarian music. In brief —we are not far from the 'starting-point'. Work, learn; work, learn; and—for the third time—work, learn. In this way we can achieve something. For if we compare Hungarian folk-music with that of other peoples, we reach a surprisingly favourable conclusion. So far as I know the music of foreign peoples, ours is far and away superior in respect of power of expression and variety. A peasant who composes a melody like the one enclosed could surely produce distinguished, first-rate things if in his childhood he could have got away from the ranks of the peasantry and studied.

[1] Budapest newspapers of the day.

44

Unfortunately the music example referred to is lost. But from the last sentence of this letter we may gather that he had already had his first encounter with Hungarian folksong.

Bartók, otherwise taciturn in his correspondence, goes on to put questions of conscience:

It is odd that the Bible supposes: 'The body is mortal, the soul immortal', when this statement changed as follows is also true, 'The body (material) is infinite, the soul (the form of the body) is finite'.

It is odd that the situations of priest and actor are generally taken to be opposite, whereas priest and actor do the same thing—tell fables.

Bartók was consistent in these views until his death. It is interesting that during his Paris visit he took no notice of Debussy. It was somewhat later, encouraged by Zoltán Kodály, that he first turned his attention to the great French impressionist.

On 10th September he was still in Paris, enjoying much sight-seeing, and other experiences. He was also absorbed in his own problems. In one letter to his mother he said that he was determined always to stay alone:

I am deserted! . . . And, knowing it, prophesy that from this time on this solitude of soul will be my fate. I seek for an ideal companion, but I know that I search in vain. If at any time I could find someone the disappointment would be quickly alleviated.

Sometimes I feel for a little while that I am on a hill. Then I take a mighty fall, and, once again I am fighting and striving. And that goes on over and over again. One day I shall be able to stay on top.

The last optimistic sentence allows one to conclude, perhaps, that Bartók's failure in Paris somewhat strengthened him to follow his own path with greater determination.

He began a new and splendid work, his First Suite, for large orchestra. This work is full of the freshness of youth, and its effectiveness is in no way lost on the contemporary listener. The first movement contains the germ of all the themes which in more or less altered form run through the whole work. The opening theme:

provides a festal opening for a colourful tone-painting that rejoices in and never tires of its varied hues. The second theme:

contrasts with the first, but is also related to it (see *a*). The third theme is similar to the first, and the fourth to the second:

The second movement is based on the second quotation above:

and it prevails throughout this section which introduces a series of other melodies of contrasting character.

The third movement grows out of themes 1 and 3:

The fourth movement begins with a theme that appears to be derived from a variant, in minor tonality, of the first.

The fifth and last movement has a principal subject that is related to the second of the themes on p. 46.

In this movement, however, the introductory theme is heard, and in this way the unity of the work is assured.

The manuscript of this work is dated 'Vienna, 1905'. The

first performance of the Suite took place in Vienna on 29th November of that year. There were, in fact, only four movements played at the first performance, which was under the auspices of the Vienna Concert Society and conducted by Ferdinand Löwe (1865–1925).

5   Hungarian folksong

One result of the political and social conditions of the first part of the nineteenth century was the division of Hungarian music between two factions. The middle classes looked towards Western Europe, particularly to the Viennese Classics and the German Romantics. Composers such as Debussy and Mussorgsky were to remain unknown for some time longer, while Hungarian composers did all they could to emulate those of Austria and Germany. The second, and rather larger, faction comprised some of the lesser and some of the greater nobility. They could not be described as connoisseurs of music, except in so far as music made an enjoyable accompaniment to food and wine. Such music was 'gipsy music', adapted for the most part from the popular ballads of the dilettanti, and to a lesser extent from the *verbunkos* music of the time of the Rákóczi uprising.

Bartók and Kodály recognized this situation, and so did other like-minded artists, and sought a way out. Inspired by the folk-music of Hungary they endeavoured to realize its artistic potentialities. It is their great merit that through so doing they brought the independent musical culture of Hungary to such a state that it could in the end stand beside the highly developed art music of Europe. At this point Bartók's objectivity in respect of popular song must be stressed. Because of his scholarly experience he had to make a sharp distinction between this (which had no foundation in folk-art) and folksong. He did not totally repudiate it, however, but assigned it to its proper place—outside the folk-art category—in accordance with scientific principles and its social function.

How was it that Bartók came to research in the field of Hungarian peasant song? In 1896 Béla Vikár (1859–1945), a distinguished expert in the field of Hungarian folk-poetry, began to assemble his epoch-making collection of folksongs. He was no musician and incapable of distinguishing between the imitation folksong and the real thing, although he was much better qualified to discriminate in regard to poetry. When he began to collect melodies, however, he arrived at the correct conclusion, that in the folk tradition words and melody were so bound together that they were indivisible. It is especially worthy of notice that Kodály, when working in this field, was one of the first to become aware of Vikár's activity, for through his work on Hungarian philology he first brought the larger issues and the consequent broadening of Vikár's collecting activity into the province of music. This foundation was not at once available to Bartók, who first undertook research into the songs of the peasants on Kodály's advice.

Bartók himself described his encounter with folk-music and with Zoltán Kodály as follows:

Not long afterwards—because I got a grant in 1905, at the restless age of twenty-four—I was seized with the desire to travel. So I began to explore Hungary. As I went from village to village I heard the true music of my race—folk-music. This was just the stimulus I needed. This music was a revelation to me. I was completely taken by surprise. I had the feeling that these wonderful, pentatonic melodies came from a forgotten age. They were several centuries old. Probably I heard them when I accidentally met Zoltán Kodály during a folksong collecting expedition, and they caused us to continue the excursion together in order to note down the old folksongs of Hungary. To this we gave all our energy so that we could discover a genuine Hungarian style.

This brought my *Sturm und Drang* period to an end. I found my vocation. You know that musical Romanticism at the beginning of the century was at its end. People were already sated with this kind of music and were beginning to look at other kinds. This was, naturally, partly a conscious, and partly an unconscious, attitude.

At this time I buried myself in the folk-music of the Slovak and Rumanian peasantry just as much as in that of the Hungarian. I wanted to do two things: to bring back the spirit of folksong, and to harmonize the melodies in modern style. I tried to make them easy to play on the piano, and, although I made use of modern means of expression, not to take away their national flavour. It was presenting the past in the mode of expression of the present, like a Hamlet in contemporary costume.[1]

The friendship between Kodály and Bartók grew closer on the foundation of their common labours. They took turns in transcribing the melodies on Vikár's phonograph rolls, and continually exchanged their experiences. To the folksong collector during the first decade of the twentieth century Hungary afforded immeasurable opportunity. It is true that the isolated medieval pattern of life of the peasantry had slowly changed after the gradual investment of capital in agriculture after the Compromise of 1867; but peasant culture remained as it always had been, although economic and political conditions were completely altered. Nevertheless when Bartók and Kodály began their joint activity it was the last possible moment, for the oldest reputable songs were even then only to be found among the oldest people. To get to know the musical speech of the Hungarian people as thoroughly as possible, one had to move fast. When, in 1950, Kodály and Gyula Kertész (b. 1900, music teacher and

[1] S. Andras Szöllősy, 'Bartók Documents', from *Üj Zenei Szemle*, March 1925.

organist) once more looked for a particular place in which Bartók had once worked they found that the store of folk-songs had noticeably diminished—one of the few negative results of the close connection between town and country of those days.

At first, expeditions in search of folk-music were intended only to serve the interests of Bartók and Kodály as composers, for they sought fresh creative stimulus from the indigenous musical culture of Hungary. Only later was the material that had been collected put into systematic order, providing one of the foundations of musical folklore.

On one occasion Béla Balázs and Bartók went into one of the Hungarian provinces in search of folksongs. (Bartók usually had a companion on his trips through villages and hamlets, as he liked it that way.) They agreed on a division of the work: Bartók took charge of the melodies, Balázs of the words. One Sunday they arrived in a village, and made a bee-line for the inn, where they found people singing for all they were worth. The bar in a village inn is not particularly roomy, and has only some four or five tables—with a few people at each. On this occasion there were some farm labourers, and other fellows, all more or less under the influence of alcohol, bawling out at the top of their voices. Naturally each group sang differently from, and was intent on singing louder than, every other. Quite imperturbable, Bartók took out his manuscript paper and began to write. Since every song had a number of verses he succeeded in transcribing four or five melodies after hearing several verses of each. At first he put down a number of note-groups from each song which he expanded when he had heard the melody repeated several times. Unfortunately Balázs could not do this with the words, for these, of course, varied from verse to verse.

Folksongs, however, were not only picked up in village

inns. It was always the oldest inhabitants of the villages who knew the most and best songs. In a letter of 16th August 1907, to Stefi Geyer, Bartók described with much humour the process of collecting songs in Transylvania. He also showed how unbelievably difficult it was to bring to light these treasures of the people, and to protect songs of great antiquity from oblivion. In general he was a man of few words, who had great difficulty in thawing and making friends. But when he was working on folksong he was very accessible and used to ask for things in so charming a manner ('for *my* sake') that it was practically impossible to resist him. By now (i.e. 1907) he had worked out a system. First he noted the melodic outline of a song, then the rhythm, and finally the words. Then he added relevant dates and other remarks.

Béla Balázs's *Reminiscences*, however, do not record the most important things that happened. Balázs was a poet of some significance, but no musician. We learn something from Pál Bodon, who accompanied Bartók to Transylvania on a folksong expedition in 1907 in order to give what help he could on the musical side. His recollections show Bartók in a quite different light and furnish some facts which, if incidental, are not without their significance. This is what Bodon had to say:

In 1907 I had passed the fourth-class examination in composition. One spring day Bartók spoke to me in a corridor in the Academy, and asked if I would like to take part in an excursion to collect folksongs. I said yes—with pleasure and also curiosity—and according to Bartók's instructions went to Hódmezövásárhely in the Easter holidays to do the job. The melodies I collected—some with phonograph—I gave to Bartók. He must have been pleased, for after the end of the academic year we discussed a similar journey to Transylvania. Bartók set out some days earlier than me, and as we had arranged, was waiting for me one day at the beginning of July on the railway station at Brassó. As I got out of the train and saw him—complete with hiking equipment—I was, at least for a minute or two, completely bowled over by his clothes and his general appearance. He had long trousers, which were turned up inside his top-boots. In addition to his shabby jacket and battered hat he wore a threadbare brown overcoat. He had not shaved for about a week; from one side of his neck dangled a phonograph, from the other a knapsack with food. At that time the modern rucksack had not yet come into use. During our trip I was frequently convinced that Bartók's outfit was entirely practical.

We went to Mádéfalva by train, and from there on 7th July travelled on to the valley of Gyimes. Mostly we walked, only taking a carriage on the way back. We began looking for folksongs as soon as we reached Mádéfalva. After our diversion to Gyimes we returned to Mádéfalva, and from there we went northwards on foot through the valley of the Olt as far as Gyergyószentmiklós. For the whole of our excursion we split up during the day, working in neighbouring communities, and met at some prearranged rendezvous in the evening to exchange notes on the day's happenings. Bartók was quite natural as a travelling companion, but, since he was a man of limited conversation, we always talked over the business in hand. It only happened once—we were resting outside at sundown at the foot of the Hargita—that Bartók was moved by the beauty of the view to break a long silence and to say: 'It would be nice to live here.'

Bartók's method of collecting folksongs comprised the most precise notation possible of the melodies; a careful indication of any clues as to date; and the exact recording of day and place of performance. Years later, in 1936, when folksong research had been more definitely formulated, he wrote:

The ideal collector of folksong must be a true polyhistorian. He must have a knowledge of speech and phonetics in order to notice and record the smallest nuances of dialect. A general knowledge of folklore makes it possible for him to establish in exact detail the relationship between folk-music and folk-custom. He needs to be a sociologist, so that he may check the changes effected by the collective life of the village and introduced into folk-music. When he has arrived at finality in these respects, he must bring historical knowledge, above all knowledge of the history of particular communities, into play. If he wants to compare the folk-music of his own country with that of others he must have knowledge of foreign languages. Above all, and unconditionally, he must be a musician, with a good ear and a talent for observation.

Bartók himself approximated to this type of many-sided scholar. For the rest, he noted in the same essay: 'As far as I know, a folksong collector of such ability, with so much knowledge and experience does not yet, and perhaps never will, exist.'

These first journeys very soon produced practical results. At the beginning of 1906 Bartók and Kodály began to assemble material for publication in one volume. Bartók himself brought together contributions, great and small, and as we know from his letters he let no opportunity go by for considering the material prerequisites for such publication. The plans reached realization, and in 1906 a volume of twenty folksongs, with simple piano accompaniment, was issued by the firm of Rózsavölgyi. Bartók was responsible for harmonizing the first ten, Kodály for the remainder. The Foreword was Kodály's, but was also signed by Bartók. It included the following points:

One must choose from the best and make it familiar to the public by means of some arrangement. What comes from the country into the town needs to be clothed. Whether arranged for choir or piano the accompaniment must serve only as a replacement for the field and the village that have been left behind.

Hungarian folksong in the concert-hall! That it will be compared with the masterpieces of world literature and with foreign folksong sounds an odd idea today. But its time will come. That is, provided that there is Hungarian music for the home, and that Hungarians cease to be satisfied with worthless foreign ditties and mass-produced stuff from our own folksong factories. Provided too that there are Hungarian singers, and that it is not only a number of connoisseurs of rarities who are aware of the existence of folksongs other than *Lari-fari* and *Dear Henry*.[1]

There is also the following note on performance:

No one who is acquainted with the manner of singing of the people will make mistakes in performing folksongs. Nor will anyone who speaks good Hungarian make major errors. This already is the half of good singing. . . . Variations from customary accentuation are not wrong, since the people never sing anything that destroys their natural feeling for speech-rhythm. Mistakes in rhythm will occur only when alien musical phrasing is imposed on the text. In this connection we could make the instructive observation that the people have made alterations in many German-style melodies that have come to us in order to fit them to the words.

Bartók's first arrangements of folksongs appeared under the title of *Three Folk-Songs from Csík County*. Here too he departed from the hitherto customary manner in that in his arrangement he underlined original tonality of the folk melodies and did not clothe them in central European harmonies. All this work made him aware of the fact that he had found in folksong a field of activity that complemented his vocation as a composer. The many discoveries he had been able to make spurred him on to a still greater effort. But the way to the realization of a truly national Hungarian music for the twentieth century was long, and many things had effectively to be brought to bear before he could reach this goal. He was always conscious that folk-music could only be a point of departure for a composer, a stimulus to the creation of music in the larger forms: 'Folk music has artistic significance only if, in the hands of a great creative artist, it can

[1] Two popular mock-folksongs.

penetrate and influence music as a liberal art.' It is characteristic of Bartók that he did not limit himself to research into Hungarian folksongs but took an interest also in those of the minorities living in Hungary—Slovaks and Rumanians—as well as of Arab, Turkish and Asiatic peoples. His passionate sense of patriotism in no way involved a disregard of other peoples and nationalities, but was derived from a deep-lying recognition of humanist values. As he said himself: 'The real keynote of my life . . . is the concept of the brotherhood of peoples—brotherhood in spite of every war, every dissension. So far as I have the strength I try to serve this ideal in my music.'

6 Professor at the Academy of Music

Bartók's efforts in research brought about a turning-point in the musical history of Hungary, but they afforded no possibility of a livelihood for him. He had, therefore, to return to piano-playing, with which, together with teaching and certain allowances, he tried to ensure an income. He did not like appearing in public, since he always believed that his memory, although it never let him down, was not entirely secure. There was, perhaps, a more serious reason for his disinclination. This was the time-taking preparation for a concert, which kept him away from composition. Already he considered this as his proper task in life.

Bartók's concert tour through Spain and Portugal with the thirteen-year-old prodigy, Ferenc von Vécsey—unwillingly undertaken in 1906 because it offered a means of earning money—should be mentioned. The most important stops in this tour were at Madrid, Lisbon and Oporto, in the last of which towns he met Camille Saint-Saëns (1835–1921). Although this tour brought in little in the material sense, since Bartók's role was solely that of accompanist, it left many impressions on his artistic sensibility. Full of enthusiasm, he wrote to his mother describing the sights of this distant part of the world:

Lisbon is a most beautiful little town, but not good for the nerves. The noise in the streets is unbelievable. Everybody offers his wares for sale at the top of his voice. There are masses of barrows about! All laden with goods. In many parts of the town the dirt is terrible.

And what sort of people they are, limping about in rags and loafing in this dirt that smells of fish. But the general impression is unbelievably friendly. In other places the sun does not shine so ingratiatingly, and this, therefore, makes the narrowest and most crooked lanes pleasant. A unique sort of town. To be sure there are no particular art treasures, but the character of the place is quite different from that of any other town I have seen. Half-African. And the brown-skinned people with pitch-black hair! Most interesting.

In comparison Madrid is nothing! Like Budapest—with a Danube shore, but no Parliament building: Madrid is hardly different from any other average large town.

Bartók made use of a free day to pay a visit to the African continent. On 18th May 1906 he went to Tangiers for some hours. He later recounted to his friend Balázs how something that he saw happen in an African inn had a special significance for him:

I had the opportunity to make an expedition to the shores of Africa. When I was there I heard Arabian songs in some Arabian tavern or other. These were very interesting. Since then I intend to go into these things. But one cannot understand a folksong without understanding the language.

Later on he put his idea into practice when, in 1913, he undertook a folksong expedition to North Africa (see p. 91). In the middle of May his concert tour in the Iberian peninsula ended. On his way home he visited the World Exhibition in Venice, and on 26th May wrote to his mother: 'On my Spanish trip I saw what is the most beautiful—in Venice. Heavenly!'

In December 1907 the longed-for turning-point in Bartók's life came. I quote from the Year Book of the Academy of Music:

In December of this academic year, in consequence of a severe illness which seized him after long years of work, Professor Thomán sought retirement. The Ministry acceded to the request of the sick professor and duly acknowledged the success of his teaching career. Our Institute has lost in him a teacher of the greatest authority and distinction, honoured as master by a great number of pupils. Among these are world-famous artists who through their zeal and conscientiousness have made their contribution to the reputation of the Academy of Music. The Ministry of Culture have appointed to succeed him Béla Bartók, former student of the Institute who is already a famous artist.

The appointment of one so young to the Academy was unprecedented. It is probable that Mrs Gruber, who had often spoken with Mihalovich about the invigoration of Hungarian music through youthful energy, had something to do with the decision. Strictly speaking, two former pupils of Thomán came under consideration for his post: Béla Bartók and Arnold Székely. Both were of an age and both already had much to show in the way of success.

Instrumental teaching, including the piano, was at that time divided into two classes. The duty of the teacher of the first, the preparatory course, was 'to give instrumental training to the students so that they should be ready to undertake the advanced ("academic") course'. The Year Book went on to describe the latter course as one which 'gave theoretical and practical instruction directed towards a perfomer's career'. After successful completion of this course, and the seminar in piano, students were awarded a State diploma. Bartók was given charge of the advanced course, Székely of the preparatory course. In this way, Bartók's material cares, for the time being, were lightened. His new post did not offer a spectacular income, but it did give him the chance of travel during the summer. He needed the vacations, partly to recover from the year's routine, partly for composition. For this he most of all needed solitude. And here it may be informative to take note of Bartók's working method.

First he made short sketches which, in general, were intelligible only to himself. These sketches reflect the actual process of creation. According to Bartók the rest of the work, needing less concentration than the first phase of composition, only required the skill of a craftsman. In this connection the following incident is relevant. Izor Kner, a well-known publisher, once met Bartók in a railway train. The composer sat in a corner of the apartment with a small flat case on his knee. Manuscript paper lay on the top of the case. Bartók, working on a score, was busily writing. (Kner clearly thought that Bartók was composing, whereas in all probability he was orchestrating.) Kner asked him if it were generally possible to compose during a railway journey. Bartók answered: 'That depends on the springs. Modern railway carriages are already so well sprung that the most severe jolts are noticeably lessened, and this enables one to write music when travelling.'

During his student years Bartók had little free time for composition. It is understandable, therefore, that this gave him small cause for satisfaction, since he considered composition and collecting folksongs as his main tasks. However, his unrivalled sense of duty did not allow him to execute his teaching commitments merely superficially. He was a first-class teacher and attended to the smallest detail, from fingering to colour and phrasing. He was particularly inclined to the music of Scarlatti, Bach, Beethoven, Liszt and Debussy. When he played Mozart he was, perhaps, too aristocratic and too delicate. He had a strong feeling for Chopin: he did not interpret his music after the 'salon' manner then customary but rather revealed facets of his work which were still unrecognized at the time. He also gave masterly interpretations of Brahms's piano works.

Bartók's teaching had one other important consequence—the issue of a whole series of classical compositions edited by him. These comprised 13 easy pieces and the *Well-tempered*

Clavier of Bach; 7 Bagatelles (Op. 33), 15 Variations (Op. 35), Polonaise (Op. 89), 11 new Bagatelles (Op. 119), and Sonatas and Écossaises by Beethoven; Chopin's Waltzes; 18 pieces by Couperin; 19 of Haydn's Sonatas; Sonatas by Mozart, as well as the Fantasie in C minor (K.396), and the *Rondo alla turca* from the A major Piano Sonata (K.331); Sonatas by Scarlatti; and two Scherzi of Schubert. He also made piano arrangements of organ works by Bach, Azzolino, della Ciaja, Frescobaldi, Benedetto Marcello, Michele Rossi and Domenico Zipoli.

A year after Bartók was appointed Professor, Zóltan Kodály was also taken on the staff of the Academy of Music and in the same year the new building of the Academy was ready for occupation. The opening ceremonies began on 12th May 1907; members of the Government—with the Prime Minister, Sándor Wekerle, at their head—took part. In his address the then Minister of Culture, Count Albert Apponyi, spoke as follows: 'Music will enjoy greater consideration than previously ..., when on account of political and social factors, it did not receive as much support as, for example, the Fine Arts. This imbalance must be corrected; but not to the disadvantage of the other arts and their permanent support, but in such a way that music may be assisted in similar manner.' He also said: 'We produce music; but now we take into account the extension of its cultivation by our people.' These were fine words and promises, but that was about all there was to it.

During the celebrations, which lasted until 18th May, Bartók appeared both as composer and pianist. As the final item of the orchestral concert on 15th May the first, second and fifth movements of the first Orchestral Suite were played. The *Pesti Hirlap* carried this report:

The greater part of the audience unfortunately left too soon, and those who stayed heard the work in a state of virtual exhaustion, or at least with stunted apperception. But this marvellous work, which is composed in an almost new Hungarian style, deserved unsparing attention. We hope, however, that the Philharmonic will make compensation to the talented composer . . . whose abilities are only surpassed by his modesty.

The hope that Bartók's Suite might be performed under more favourable conditions during the next concert season was unfortunately not realized. It was not performed again until 1st March 1909, conducted by Jenő von Hubay. This was, in fact, the first complete performance in Hungary.

During 1907 Bartók's thoughts were turned inward, and it was a time of decision; for it was at this time that the crisis occurred which finally resulted in the style of composition which today we describe as 'Bartókian'. There is evidence to support this in a letter to Stefi Geyer, a violinist scarcely twenty years old, but whose reputation at the time was considerable. In this letter Bartók exposed a much stronger basis to his atheism than before. This may have been due to the fact that Stefi herself was a sincere religious believer. The spirit of contradiction, which was always alive in Bartók, spoke out now with unusual force:

The Bible tells us with wonderful consistency the exact opposite of the truth of this world: for it is not that God has made man in his own image and likeness, but that man made God after his image. It is not the body that is mortal and the soul immortal, but precisely the other way round: the soul is transient and the body (i.e. the material) eternal! Why are so many millions of people stuffed with false sayings, so that the majority hold on to them until death? The minority, however, after struggles which could also be rendered superfluous, free themselves from them! It is easier to deal with virgin soil rather than with that which already has weeds sown in it.

This struggle which was imposed on me by the order of the

world, followed this course. Until I was fourteen years old as an earnest Catholic I respected 'authority'. I was deeply upset by the fact that political reforms were introduced at that time and civil marriage was instituted, which weakened the power of the Church. When we were 15 or 16 we learned (in religious instruction) the complete moral scheme, the ceremonies, the dogmas, and the history of the Church; and, indeed, since we had a zealous and energetic teacher, much more than what was prescribed. You cannot imagine what detail we went into in the individual sections. For instance, in the field of morals we had to answer such questions as this: If a man's wife and his parents all fall into a river, who must he rescue first? We also learned this 'important' case: that if anyone is allowed to eat meat on Fridays because of episcopal relaxation, he is not allowed on the other hand to eat fish on Fridays so long as the episcopal relaxation remains in operation. We also learned of the compassion of the Church; how, for example, it is forbidden to anyone, by papal decree, to entertain a heretic in his house and to supply him with food on pain of excommunication. (I, for example, am such a heretic.) Our zealous teacher was brilliantly successful, so that since that time in principle I have been no Catholic. The problem of 'God' and the 'immortal soul' for the time being I left in suspense, moving neither backwards nor forwards. When I was eighteen, free from the yoke of school, I had time to read more serious books. Later my studies in astronomy, the books of a Danish writer, an acquaintance, and particularly my own reflections, all greatly impressed me. By the time I was twenty-three I was a new man—an atheist.... Ah! I would not write about this—but only in melancholy, inoffensive strains without discord. But in the end I arrived at a state of violence. My kingdom is one of discord!

The letter ends: 'Greetings from a godless man (who is more honest than most of the godly).'

This letter gives an idea of Bartók's inner struggles, of the tumult in his soul. It is particularly interesting to read what he has to say about discord. Here, perhaps, we may find an approach to the style of his music at that time, which was subsequently further developed. It was seldom that he either wrote or spoke as he did in this letter, which gives it a special importance. From it we also learn that Stefi Geyer played some part in his music. He wrote a melancholy tune and over a four-note motive within it inscribed these words: 'This is your *Leitmotiv.*'

This *Leitmotiv* occurs in a number of Bartók's compositions, with especial frequency in those of 1908, to which we shall return (see pp. 68 ff.).

In 1907 Bartók got to know Debussy's works, about which he wrote in his autobiography:

As . . . at Kodály's instigation, I became acquainted with and studied Debussy's works I noticed with astonishment that certain pentatonic traits analogous to those in our folk-music played a role in his melodies. Doubtless those are also to be attributed to the influence of Eastern European folk-music—probably Russian.

This may be expanded by the following extract from an article on the subject of folk-music and the new music of Hungary:

Already in 1905 I ended a work in F♯ minor with this chord—F♯, A, C♯, E. In this cadence the seventh is a consonance. At this time such a cadence was unusual, but something similar may be found in several of Debussy's works of about this time in a cadence in the major—A, C♯, E, F♯. At that time, however, I did not know these compositions of Debussy.

For Bartók the encounter with Hungarian folk-music was decisive so far as the renewal of the language of music was concerned and at the same time was the last step in a long developing process. We can see the end result in his second Suite for Orchestra. In the first Suite there is no sign of the involvement of Hungarian folk-music; in the second it may be recognized for the first time. The beginnings of this work reached back as far as 1905. But after the third movement Bartók broke off and did not resume work till two years later. In the fourth, and last, movement of the work this melody is to be heard:

Here one comes across a totally different atmosphere. This melody says something that is fundamental. Bartók has discovered his native language. The inflections of folk-music here appear in Hungarian music for the first time. Today we can think of them only in conjunction with Bartók's own idiom. From that time they led directly to his greatest, truly classic, works.

Since Hungarian folk-music in its original form is monodic, a suitable harmonic scheme needed to be created. Hungarian folk melodies are based on a pentatonic scale without semitones. This scale, however, includes the intervals of major second and perfect fourth, which Bartók and Kodály treat as consonant and use in final cadences.

We return to Budapest, and to Bartók at work. In addition to his duties as professor in the Academy of Music and because he was a celebrated pianist, Bartók had a large number of private pupils. Among them were Herma and Márta Ziegler, daughters of an Inspector-General of police. Márta was very young—barely fourteen—but Bartók nevertheless paid special attention to her, for she was outstandingly musical. He was recommended to the Zieglers by a mutual acquaintance from Pressburg, and in their family circle he found peace and quiet, which a person of his temperament very much needed. In the next year—1908—he dedicated to Márta his 'Picture of a girl'—a piano piece published among his *Sketches* in 1910.

His teaching career at the Academy lasted for almost thirty years. In 1934 he was transferred to the Academy of Sciences, where finally he could dedicate himself to what lay nearest his heart—folksong research.

7   A subject of controversy

Bartók's appointment to the staff of the Academy of Music in Budapest so improved the conditions under which he lived that he was now able to concentrate entirely on one objective —the development of his creative function. Since his childhood he had always been a severe self-critic, and if at this stage he considered that all his works so far had been to a greater or lesser degree influenced by other composers, it is no cause for surprise. What now mattered was that he should open up the way for his own distinctive style, as first shown in *Two Portraits*. Both movements of this work deal with the same thematic germ, but in two different ways. The first— *Andante*—begins with the theme which Bartók had not long before described as Stefi Geyer's *Leitmotiv*:

This piece—the 'ideal likeness'—reminds one of the tonal atmosphere of *Tristan*, but it must be regarded as essentially Bartókian. A solo violin plays a decisive role, and it may be deduced that the movement was part of one of the violin concertos belonging to this period. The second movement, *Presto*, is built on the same theme, but grotesquely distorted. This is also to be found again as one of the pieces in the *Fourteen Bagatelles* for piano that were published later. The

beginning is a grotesque waltz in which the opening notes are
identical with those of the first movement:

This manner of arranging the same thematic material in
different ways goes back to Liszt. But since by this time
Bartók was aware of a large number of Hungarian folksongs
and also of the manner in which the peasants varied them, it
is reasonable to suppose that such experience helped him
towards an intensification of Liszt's procedures in variation
form. This principle became progressively more significant
in Bartók's later works.

The *Fourteen Bagatelles* are a series of pieces which already
demonstrate Bartók's new style. The individual pieces
constitute a varied miscellany and sufficiently show the experimental nature of this style. This in turn indicates, however, the crisis—both personal and artistic—which Bartók
had to overcome. There are to be found in the music bi-
tonality, linear counterpoint, chords containing more than
four different notes, and so on. But there are traces too of the
peasant music of Hungary and Slovakia that had not so long
before been discovered. These two sources of what was new
—atonality and peasant music—were just as effective as other

and better-bred ways of attacking the petty bourgeois romanticism that Bartók was more and more determined to subdue. There is also at this point the music of Debussy to be taken into account. Of this Bartók had become aware through his friend Zoltán Kodály after his return from Paris in 1907. At this time he knew relatively little of Schoenberg. He may have known the first String Quartet, but certainly not the Chamber Symphony of 1906. Yet in Nos. 8, 10 and 11 of the *Bagatelles* there are chords, built on fourths, which are ahead of anything done by Schoenberg in that Symphony. His permanent connection with folk-music, however, prevented Bartók from losing himself in such experimentation.

It is interesting to note that the *Leitmotiv* which has already been cited several times also appears in No. 13 of the *Bagatelles*. At the end of the piece—which bears the inscription 'Elle est morte'—the theme reappears thus, with the word 'meghalt' (she is dead) written above the motiv:

When he heard them played by Bartók, Busoni greatly enjoyed the *Bagatelles*. 'At last,' he observed, 'there is something that is new.' He also gave the composer a letter of recommendation to the Leipzig firm of Breitkopf & Härtel but, since they did not publish the work, this did not produce the desired effect. It finally appeared on the list of Rózsavölgyi of Budapest.

The set of *Ten easy piano pieces* probably belong to the same period of composition as the *Bagatelles*. But they are somewhat less experimental, being equable, unsensational and appropriately serious in character. The individual pieces follow one another in logical sequence. Nos. 1, 3, 6 and 8 are folksong arrangements which are set off by the contrasts of Nos. 2, 4, 7 and 9. Nos. 5 and 10 are brief recapitulations. The series begins with a 'Dedication'—with the *Leitmotiv*—that is not numbered. The best-known piece in the set is No. 10, the 'Bear's Dance', in which a typical Hungarian swineherd's dance is recollected above an *ostinato* bass. This anticipates the *Allegro Barbaro*.

We naturally come across problems of sonority and melody in both these volumes of piano pieces, but it is already Bartók's own world of music which confronts us. He declared of his own as of Kodály's music: 'Our works are in the end tonal in character. It is true that for a time I approximated to a kind of "twelve-note music", but it is wrong to assume that my music of that period was built on any particular tonal foundation'. This was in fact written in 1928, but it is applicable to the earlier period with which we are concerned.

It is interesting that at this time Bartók actually utilized two styles—one for his own compositions, and one for folksong arrangements. The blending of these two styles was the composer's main task for the next few years. For the time being, however, he determined by truly artistic means to lead the public, bred in a town environment, to a proper appreciation of folk-music. He hoped that acquaintance with folk-art would allow others to enjoy experiences similar to his own.

In the summer of 1908 Bartók travelled to France. He wrote from Argentières on 27th July: 'It is beautiful here. There is no great mass of Grand Hotels; no horde of rotten, useless, English good-for-nothings; no network of funicular railways all over the place . . . For the poor thirsty mortal there is unspoilt nature.' At this time his first works directly related to his teaching activities had appeared. Later on they

were brought together and issued under the title *For Children.*
This cycle is contained in four volumes, with eighty-five
pieces altogether. Without exception they are arrangements
of folksongs. The first two volumes contain only arrangements of Hungarian music, but, in the last two, arrangements
of Slovak music are to be found. The pieces in the cycle are
also within the capacity of pianists with no more than
moderate technical and musical endowments. At the same time
they are admirably designed to make young students familiar
with the spirit of modern music. In *For Children* Bartók's
style in harmonization for the first time shows itself in mature
form. We find that passing and auxiliary notes are not used
decoratively but as principal notes in melody and harmony.
Suspensions and secondary sevenths often appear without
preparation and mostly without resolution, while the most
important harmonic features in these pieces are the pedal
point and the *ostinato* bass. Influenced by the music of the
Hungarian peasantry, Bartók frequently utilized the 'church
modes', so that his cadences differed from those at that time
familiar in central European music.

No. 23 from the second volume may serve as an example.
Here we have to deal with three different harmonizations of
the same melody—a practice almost always followed by
Bartók in respect of repeated melodies. The first time the
tune is heard it is firmly harmonized in C major:

The next statement is based on E (minor)—or perhaps the
Phrygian mode:

The tonic of the third version is F (or perhaps B♭):

This harmonization could also be described as transposed Lydian. It will be noticed that each tonic (if we may regard it as such) appears as a pedal point. None the less it is not wrong to regard the whole piece as standing in the key of C. This example shows that while Bartók's harmonic methods were simple they were not stereotyped.

It is astonishing how, in this cycle of pieces, Bartók both appreciated and solved certain pedagogic problems with assurance. One would almost be inclined to say that the composer was clearly at that stage of his own development as a composer where he could derive from technical difficulties of common occurrence such principles as could provide the foundation for a teaching method.

In 1945, the year of Bartók's death, Boosey & Hawkes issued a revised edition of *For Children* which must be regarded as the definitive version. There are six pieces less, but the reason for their exclusion is not known. It may be that they had been wrongly transcribed in the first place, or that they were not authentic folksongs. Seven pieces—all Hungarian folksongs—have a new lay-out and fresh harmonies; one must remember that in the intervening years Bartók had enormously increased his knowledge of the tonal sphere of folk-music. This greater knowledge may also be taken to account for the appearance of patterns in the final version that were not previously to be found. Since the texts of the songs are absent from the English edition many of the titles had to be altered.

After the composition of the *Bagatelles* Bartók was engaged in an unceasing battle against conservatism and stupidity. He had inner problems to resolve as well as those that occurred in the normal course of life so that he could go forward on his own way. He shared some of his worries with his mother, as his letters to Pressburg from Budapest show. But it appears that Mrs Bartók was not able to give her son the moral support he so badly needed, and so he became alienated from her and more and more disinclined to take her counsel in respect either of musical or personal matters. One day he announced to her his intention to marry his pupil, Márta Ziegler, to whom he had already dedicated two works. It was a quiet wedding, and Mrs Bartók was present.

In Bartók's life, and also in the musical life of Hungary in the first half of this century, the Waldbauer Quartet played a prominent part. These artists rendered great service, especially in their efforts to enlarge interest in contemporary music, and were responsible for bringing to public notice the string quartets of Bartók and Kodály. It is easily understandable that Bartók should have had a cordial relationship with Waldbauer and his colleagues. He was indeed very intimate with them, and this fact was of considerable consequence for him. But whenever he attended their rehearsals he again showed the withheld, taciturn side of his nature. There are several anecdotes told about this. On one occasion Waldbauer and his fellow players, after practising for a long time, noticed that they had been consistently playing a wrong note. Having corrected their error they asked Bartók why he had not drawn their attention to it. All he said was: 'But you have found it out for yourselves.'

Meanwhile opposition to Bartók's works steadily increased. The second orchestral Suite, which was again scheduled for a concert, was once more withdrawn from the programme; on account of the conductor falling ill, so it was said. It was Busoni who always made every effort to make Bartók's way easier and to help him towards success. One day he sent a telegram asking if Bartók would be willing to conduct one movement from the Suite. Bartók at once replied that he would. So he went to Berlin and directed a performance there on 2nd January 1909. He reported to Thomán: 'It is splendid to conduct when the orchestra plays exactly as I want it to play. The result was similar to what happened in Budapest with the waltz. Two camps: one hissing, the other thundering enthusiastic applause, five times recalled . . . The orchestra is marvellous, everything sounds brilliant.'

Not long after his Berlin visit, on 27th January, he completed his first String Quartet. We can best follow the development of his style through the string quartets, each one of which marks a milestone. All the conclusions that he reached in the course of his career as a composer are brought together in the quartets. In this respect Bartók reminds one of Beethoven. Like Beethoven, in these works he expressed his most personal and innermost feelings; his quartets are his most heart-felt confessions.

The first Quartet already shows the special features of Bartók's music: plasticity of themes, masterly counterpoint, and consideration for the individuality of each instrument. It is also interesting that—as in Beethoven's Quartet in C♯ minor (Op. 131)—the first movement begins with a slow-moving subject worked out fugally:

The second movement (*Allegretto*), in spite of its extended character, is really only the preparation for the third. It ends with an introduction (*Introduzione*) to this movement, which brings the whole work to a worthy conclusion. The dance-like principal subject:

gives to the whole movement a lively, joyful character—indeed, in some places it positively brims over with exuberance.

On 1st March 1909 the first orchestral Suite was given without cuts. The *Magyar Hirlap* had this to say: 'This work of Bartók's is enchanting, popular Hungarian music ... The orchestration is dazzling, and stimulates attention all the time. At the rehearsal yesterday this five-movement work was greeted with a great show of approval, and the composer was recalled to the platform with deafening applause.' The *Pester Lloyd* critic after noting Bartók's 'powerful talent' wrote:

The work has some moments of lyrical beauty, but repellent, cacophonous distortions occur. A powerful orchestral apparatus is used almost all the time in order to surpass Richard Strauss at every point. All this is to be taken *cum grano salis*. One can see no kind of purpose in this disjointed music that goes all ways at once, and so one is more irritated. The work was played with that degree of devotion and affection of which only colleagues and pupils are capable. As was only natural the audience gave the work a mixed reception. The friends of the young radical had the upper hand, and he was recalled to the platform.

These critics—and very likely the public too—were in no doubt as to Bartók's genius, but they were also aware of his radicalism and on this account condemned him. Again and again, particularly in later criticisms, people wanted to persuade Bartók to return to a more conservative manner, in spite of his great talents being generally acknowledged. During his lifetime people did not suggest to Bartók that he should lead them to a 'better way', but sought rather to influence him to stay put on broad and well-trodden territory. Closely connected with this was the suggestion that he should give up the Hungarian element in his music.

How Bartók was to be directed to the 'correct way' by public opinion may be appreciated from the reception given to his Rhapsody for Piano and Orchestra when it was performed for the first time in November. This was a rearrangement of the work composed for the Rubinstein Competition and it was now introduced to the public in its new form. On 16th November 1909 the *Budapesti Hirlap* offered this opinion:

The laws of the theory of music, derived from harmonic and melodic design are here entirely disregarded. This is the result of the confused medley of sounds produced by the noisy orchestration. No doubt there are interesting new colours in this tonal chaos, which, if treated with a sense of proportion, might compel our interest; but going on at a stretch without any inner substance they become boring. It must be recognized, however, that Béla Bartók encompassed the difficulties of the piano part—bad enough to sprain one's wrists—with remarkable virtuosity.

Bartók's gifts and his complete individuality, therefore,

made a generally deep impression, and what resulted from them never failed to make their mark on those who heard his music—even on those unwilling to accept it. Some weeks after the performance of the Rhapsody, the Philharmonic Society, conducted by István Kerner, played the Second Suite for Orchestra. It has already been mentioned that the first three movements belonged to Bartók's earlier period, while the fourth came after he had become acquainted with Hungarian folk-music. The critics, however, had nothing to say about this, and overlooked the great change that was, so to speak, taking place before the ears of the audience. In his notice the critic of the *Pesti Napló* wrote: 'This music is a malicious and perverse freak. One can at best only be angry and grieve that such an undoubted man of genius can become victim to artistic caprice and the disease that destroys talent.'

In the summer of this year Bartók once more went on a folksong-collecting mission to Belényes where he stayed with his sister and brother-in-law. As he studied the folksongs he detected in them an alien influence. In his opinion this must have come from a Rumanian source. He wrote at once to the headmaster of the Old Catholic Grammar School in Belényes, János Buşiţia, and asked if he would help him in his researches. Buşiţia, who was well trained in music (which he taught in his school), said that he would be pleased to do so. The close friendship between these two that began at this point was able to withstand all the strains imposed on it by chauvinistic nationalism. At that time Bartók had not yet mastered the Rumanian language, and so had to get a pupil of Buşiţia to write down the words of the songs. Since Bartók believed that folksong collection was not possible without an exact knowledge of the words, he began to learn Rumanian, and was so successful that before long he could both speak and write the language. In the course of his life he collected more than 3,500 Rumanian folksongs.

In May 1911 the Rumanian Academy of Science accepted 371 Rumanian folksongs assembled by Bartók for publication. At Christmas he and his wife went to Paris—for the first time since the Rubinstein Competition of unhappy memory. Here he met among others Isidor Philipp (1863–1958). Philipp, who had come from Hungary and was Director of the Conservatoire, offered to introduce Bartók to various French musicians. He mentioned several names, but Bartók rejected them. He had only one wish: to meet Debussy. 'But he is a dreadful misanthropist,' said Philipp. 'He is sure to be churlish with you too. Do you want Debussy to insult you?' 'Yes,' said Bartók. At this time Debussy was busy with opera projects, and had more or less retired from the world. He wrote in one of his letters: 'I am incompatible with the twentieth century. I commit ten discourtesies every hour.' It is most unlikely that a meeting with Bartók took place.

In 1910 Bartók completed a new work for orchestra—*Two Portraits* (Op. 10). The first movement, with a characteristic opening, has the very appropriate title 'In full bloom'.

It begins with an effect of rustling and humming, which in Bartók is the expression of the freedom of nature. This is achieved by *tremolo* strings (without violins) and makes the

listener aware of a particular kind of atmosphere, which is
intensified with the gentle bird-song of the flute. The second
movement, which follows straight on, is described as 'Village
Dance'. Its opening theme expresses the character of some
rollicking festivity in the country:

This is music that recalls Rumanian rather than Hungarian
folk-music. The character of Rumanian music, however, is
even more marked in a piano work of this period, the *Two
Rumanian Dances*, which make great demands on the pianistic
ability of the interpreter. In spite of the title, this has nothing
directly to do with folk-music material—though all the
melodies in the two pieces certainly have a folk character—
but is entirely original.

The first *Rumanian Dance*, which Bartók himself often
liked to play, begins very softly, but with a tense rhythm:

It gradually grows louder and wilder. In the central section a
lively dance is introduced:

This is, in fact, merely an interpolation, for this melancholy part of the piece in general has nothing of the dance about it. Before long, however, the first theme reappears, and after it has ended the listener feels as if the dance yet lingers on. This work is the first which bears the mark of Bartók's fully developed mastery of the expressive power of the piano.

In this year a son was born to the Bartóks who was also named Béla.

At that time there was a group of progressive artists, painters and sculptors, known as 'the Eight', in Budapest. Róbert Berény, Károly Kernstock, Béla Czóbel and Dezső Czigány, genuine forward-looking thinkers, were members of this group, which met more or less regularly in the Palermo Café. There they used to discuss artistic and ideological matters. The most musical of the group, without doubt, was Berény, who had known Bartók since 1906. Bartók visited him frequently, and liked to play the piano—Beethoven's Sonatas mostly—to him. In 1913, very likely in April, Berény painted Bartók's portrait, which is now in New York.

'The Eight' were, among other things, responsible for an exhibition of contemporary paintings in Budapest. In the exhibition gallery the Waldbauer Quartet played quartets by Bartók and Kodály, which were introduced by Béla Balázs, at that time a notable poet and person of authority in cultural matters in Budapest. These performances helped a good deal in ensuring that Kodály and Bartók became recognized as composers. More significant, however, were the concerts, exclusively made up of their own works, which they gave in March 1910. These took place on consecutive evenings, and Bartók unselfishly devoted his pianistic talent to the cause of helping his friend.

The two concerts aroused a veritable storm of protest from the conservative part of the Budapest public, and the press started a regular campaign against the two composers. The performances of Kodály's and Bartók's works were, however, very successful so far as the Waldbauer Quartet was concerned. A Dutch concert agent immediately offered a foreign tour. Waldbauer accepted the offer, but reserved the right to include in each programme a work by a modern Hungarian composer (which meant, in the first place, the quartets of Bartók and Kodály). Bartók himself went to Switzerland and played his Rhapsody, conducted by Volkmar Andreae, at a music festival.

In this year he also gathered together many of his country's folksongs. In November he went to a small town called Ipolyság with the intention of collecting some music for bagpipes. The County Archivist, Lajos Szokoly, was willing to assist, and with his help Bartók succeeded in accumulating a large number of interesting melodies. Szokoly, among other events, organized a competitive festival for the wind-players in the village. Ten horn-players and five bagpipers turned up, and Bartók was greatly taken with the folk-costumes and the richly decorated bagpipes—a painter's delight.

István Győrffy, representing the ethnographical department of the Academy of Sciences, took part in the festival, of which he wrote the following account in the *Vasárnapi Ujság*:

The competition was not meant to be public, but the people of the little town made a great to-do about it. Hence the shepherds displayed their artistry in the Market Place. To begin with the horn-players performed by themselves. One after another they sounded the oldest horn tunes in all their purity, for the swineherds of Hont were not yet subject to the influence of the military march. Then came the bagpipers by themselves. The winners were the competitors from Hont and Ipolspásztó, the former in horn-playing, the latter in bagpiping. Phonograph recordings were not ready until the evening, at the County Hall. Those who had to wait in the court-yard naturally took the opportunity to arrange an informal dance. To the delight of the younger people some of the old swineherds danced the traditional dance of their calling to bag-pipe accompaniment. Then, during the evening, they went on a drinking spree—which a shepherd never failed to do when he came to town. So the sound of the bagpipe was heard about the town until well into the night.

In the meantime an important musical event was being prepared in Budapest, since one of the most celebrated ex-ponents of modern music, Debussy, intended to visit the capital. For weeks beforehand music-lovers and the whole of the press concerned themselves with the works of the French composer. Debussy's stay in Budapest, therefore, was a really outstanding occasion. The composer played several of his piano pieces in the large hall of the Redoute in Pest; the Waldbauer Quartet gave a performance of the String Quartet; and the Paris singer, Rose Féart, who had travelled with Debussy, sang some of his songs. Unfortunately none of his orchestral works was heard.

The playing of the Waldbauer Quartet made an especially strong impression. The third movement of Debussy's quartet was so beautiful, and given with such insight and conviction, that at the end the applause simply would not stop, and the composer had to return to the platform many times to thank the young players for their interpretation. He also invited them to visit Paris. Waldbauer and his colleagues also played Bartók's Quartet to Debussy, but he failed to appreciate it.

Modern music slowly asserted itself abroad; it was only in Hungary that it could gain no ground. The principal reason for this may very well have been that contemporary works were indifferently interpreted, whereas music of this kind demands a faultless performance. Thus the right conditions had to be created. At the beginning of 1911 several young musicians—Bartók and Kodály among them—founded the New Hungarian Music Society, the main duty of which was

83

to introduce contemporary music to the public through impeccable performances. Bartók wrote about this in his autobiography:

My works from Opus 4 onwards, which were meant to express exactly the ideas described, understandably aroused much opposition in Budapest. One reason for this was, that with us the performance of new orchestral works was almost always unsatisfactory, since neither a perceptive conductor nor the right orchestra was available. When the struggle became particularly critical in 1911, a group of young musicians, including Kodály and myself, attempted to set up a New Hungarian Music Society. The real purpose of this was to organize an independent orchestra, which could give decent performances of older music, as well as of more recent and completely new works.

The establishment of an orchestra, however, was not the only aim of the new society; it also aimed at organizing recitals and lectures. The orchestra failed to come into existence because there was never any chance of getting financial backing. Nor could the magazine that was planned appear. Nevertheless, in spite of everything, the new society soon began to work. In November 1911 the first concert took place—a recital by Bartók. He played pieces by Couperin, Rameau and Domenico Scarlatti, as well as Beethoven's *Variations on a theme of Righini*, which is seldom heard. In another concert Dezső Róna sang Hungarian folksongs arranged by Kodály and Bartók, but it seems that these did not live up to the claims made for them and they fell rather flat. On this occasion Bartók devoted his pianistic skills to his own infrequently heard pieces. He enjoyed much success even though the audience was very small—about 100 or 150, certainly no more. Those who were there, however, went home the richer for their experience.

About two weeks later the society gave another concert,

Béla Bartók in youth

István Thomán with a group of pupils. *Front row: Thomán (centre),
Felicitas Fábián (second from right); second row, from left: Arnold
Székely, Sari Erkel (grand-daughter of Ferenc Erkel), Béla Bartók*

Manuscript of the Symphonic Poem, *Kossuth*

Setting for the first performance of *Bluebeard's Castle*

Bartók and his second wife, Ditta Pásztory

Broadcasting a talk on Hungarian folk-music, Budapest

Bartók, 1936

Bartók, 1936

of contemporary music, with works by Leó Weiner, Ravel and Debussy. The audience was even smaller than on the previous occasion. In January and March of the following year further concerts were organized, but through lack of interest the society regrettably had to suspend operations and go into liquidation. Lack of success and indifference, which Bartók met on all sides, depressed him so much that he seriously entertained thoughts of emigration. The year 1911 may be described as the most bitter, and the saddest, period of his life. He withdrew from public musical activity, but returned with even greater energy to the study of folklore.

It has already been mentioned that the music critics of the time were anxious at all costs to lead Bartók to the 'way of improvement' and to set him on the 'return' journey. A volume of Hungarian music published in 1910 for the foreign market shows how he should have 'returned'. Bartók was represented by *Three Folk-songs from Csík County*. But in what company! The other composers in the collection were: Kern, Szendy, Weiner, Buttykay, Rezső Lavotta, Siklós, Dienzl, Jacobi, Aggházy, Chován and Zichy. At that time these were accepted as the representatives of modern Hungarian music.

Bartók's only opera, *Duke Bluebeard's Castle*, was composed at this time. Béla Balázs had actually written the libretto for Kodály, who, however, said that he had no time to deal with it and proposed that it should be shown to Bartók. Mrs Gruber, who in the meantime had married Kodály, brought Bartók and Balázs together and, after reading the libretto, the former declared his willingness to set it to music. It was his first opera and was to be his last.

Before the curtain rises a bard speaks the Prologue at the end of which we hear as a background a pentatonic motive, like a folksong, which prepares the audience for the sombre, mystical mood of the opera:

Bartók

When the curtain goes up we see a dark Gothic hall, with
only one small iron door at the top of a staircase and seven
great iron doors let into the walls. The impenetrable gloom
is first broken when the small door opens and Duke Bluebeard and Judith come down the staircase illuminated by a
shaft of light. Judith has forsaken parents, brothers and lovers
to go with Bluebeard into his dark and mysterious stronghold.
As she hesitates to go down into the gloom of the hall Bluebeard tells her that she may go back whence she came; but
although aware that he is 'many times outlawed' she is ready
to give up everything to follow him. The door closes behind
her. In the gloom that once again prevails she runs her hands
along the walls, which are damp—damp, as she believes, from
tears. Bluebeard describes the beauty of the sunny, golden
chambers of love; but Judith replies, 'Desist, you who have
been so often deserted.' With growing ardour she says that
she will bring light and warmth into Bluebeard's Castle.
Impetuously she demands that he should open the seven
locked doors for her. He gives her the key of the first, and as
she opens it a red glow shines into the hall. She is looking
into Bluebeard's torture-chamber. At the same time she discovers that it is not tears but blood that makes the walls damp.
For the first time the 'blood motiv' sounds in the orchestra:

86

In spite of her terror, Judith finds herself able to appreciate the light that comes into the hall through the open door. One after the other she takes the keys of the other rooms, and ever more light breaks forth. She looks into Bluebeard's armoury—with blood on the weapons; into his treasury—the jewellery is bloody too; and into his magic garden, where this characteristic chord occurs:

In the garden the earth is soaked with blood. From an alcove she looks out over Bluebeard's land, over which a cloud throws bloody shadows. Bluebeard thanks Judith for the flood of light she has brought into his castle. But she sees only the doors which are still shut, the keys of which Bluebeard keeps from her, because it cannot now become any brighter. Judith, however, is determined to get to the bottom of Bluebeard's last secret, and she opens the next to last door. Before her a white lake is spread out—the Lake of Tears. Its reflection extends over the hall, like a shadow, and is expressed in the music of the 'tear-motiv':

Bluebeard demands Judith's unquestioning love, but she insists on knowing if he has loved anyone before her. This secret is kept behind the seventh door: the silver light of the moon falls into the hall, and in it three beautiful, pale women walk across to Judith. These are the women that Bluebeard loved before he loved her.

Bluebeard falls on his knees and speaks of them—of when he discovered each one, of his thoughts on each—as in a dream. Every morning belongs to the first, every afternoon to the second, every evening to the third. 'At last I found the fourth at night—at night by the bright heavenly stars. The whiteness of your face was my illumination. Your brown hair drove the clouds away; from henceforth every night is yours.' Of all his wives Judith was the loveliest. Bluebeard adorns her with mantle and crown, and she follows the women into the seventh chamber. Around him falls eternal night.

Béla Balázs wrote an article about his libretto and said that he had 'tried to fashion modern, intellectual experiences from the raw material of the Székely folk-ballads'. This, together with the fact that the poem appeared in a volume entitled *Mysteries*, shows that Balázs at the time paid homage to the tendency fashionable at the time, towards mysticism. However, he soon detached himself from such ideas. *Duke Bluebeard's Castle* in fact contains many elements from the world of the old Hungarian folk-ballads. At the same time the subject is entirely modern: the inescapable loneliness of man. Who but Bartók, who remained a solitary among artists and men until the end, could have set this subject to music? In Balázs's allegory Bluebeard's fortune depends on the person whom he loves, but whom finally he can treasure only in his innermost thoughts and his memories. He can never reach fulfilment.

When Bartók had completed the work there was no prospect of performance. He wrote *Duke Bluebeard's Castle* in the first place for himself and for the future, when it might become possible for modern Hungarian music to be given to the public.

In a piano work that belongs to the same creative period there is a completely different attitude. This is the *Allegro Barbaro*, in which for the first time in Bartók's work Hungarian folk-music and twentieth-century idioms are united. The fierce power that comes from the strong, positive melody built on the chord of F♯ minor is typically Magyar:

The problem of form is also solved in a new way. The work may be described as a rondo, but the order of the themes and their modification as they recur is the product of Bartók's original invention, which cannot be forced into any formal pattern. Another short piano piece of the same period is the second of the *Three Burlesques*, which collectively became Opus 8. The piece, which is marked 'a little excited', shows in the use of the interval of the fourth in the melody a characteristic of folksong developed in a twentieth-century composition:

The cycle of *Four Pieces for Orchestra* also belongs to this period.

In 1912 Bartók was commissioned by the firm of Rózsa-völgyi & Co. to write a new 'Piano Method'. At first he hesitated to undertake this commission, but finally agreed on condition that he was allowed the collaboration of a music-teacher who was at the same time a composer. The publisher having consented to this, Bartók invited a junior colleague, Sándor Reschofsky, to work with him on the project. Reschofsky put the plan of the 'Piano Method' together, and Bartók wrote some of the exercises, the rest being composed by Reschofsky. Each piece was designed to serve a particular technical end, such as fingering, position of the hands, etc. To solve such problems was by no means an easy task. Bartók often found himself in a state of doubt and the task weighed heavy on him. From time to time, having written a piece, he had to re-write it because its particular aim had not been ful-filled. Nevertheless, in spite of all the difficulties, he learned a lot from this work and gained a good deal of experience. Some of the solutions to technical problems given in these pieces are to be found again in *Mikrokosmos*. The *Bartók-Reschofsky Piano Method* did not become very popular, for piano-teachers were not able to appreciate a new scheme based on the principles of modern music. Chován and Szendy, the two chief representatives of the old school of piano-teaching, were particularly loth to have anything to do with the kind of instruction put forward in this work. Some of Bartók's pieces were later issued separately under the title, *The first term at the piano*.

In the summer of 1912 Bartók and his wife visited Norway. In the autumn he wrote a postcard to his friend Buşiţia, in Bucharest, which was also signed by Dimitre Kiriac (1861–1923), a Rumanian composer and conductor whom he had got to know through his work on Rumanian folksong. His next summer holidays he planned to spend in North Africa, in order to study the folk-music of the Arabs. On 1st April

1913 he wrote a letter to Géza Vilmos Zágon (1890–1918), composer and writer on music, in which he said:

This summer, i.e. in June and July, I would like to go to Algiers (to be precise, somewhere near Biskra, and later to the Kabyles) to collect Arab and Berber folk-music (with phonograph, of course). I sent a request to the Ministry of Culture, in which I asked that an official letter of recommendation should be procured from the French Minister of the Interior for the Algerian authorities. From the Ministry of Culture I had the cheering news that the French would not give us one (on political grounds!). Actually, in the middle of February the request went to the Ministry of Foreign Affairs, and as yet there is no news of anything being settled; so there is little hope of success. I had the idea that I might be able to get a note of recommendation as a 'correspondent' from one of the Budapest newspapers (with which special correspondents can travel all over the world, to theatres of war, etc.). Several of them remarked that I might prefer to apply to Paris.[1]

It seems that Zágon took it upon himself to facilitate this matter, since Bartók placed the correspondence before him. On 3rd May he wrote again about the African journey:

The heat doesn't worry me. The maximum temperature in Biskra is said to be 48° C. (in the shade). But in June it can hardly rise to this. Then, I can rest during the hottest time of day, since the morning and evening will do for working. Considering that in Hungary it can also be 40° C. in the shade—which is all right, even delightful, for me—I am not in the least concerned about the heat.

The formalities were completed and the Bartóks were able to undertake their journey. On 19th June Bartók sent a post-card to Zágon:

I have now been collecting in the villages in the oases for eight days and, thanks to the letter of recommendation, it is easier to

[1] This letter was published by György Bella in the journal *Csillag* (July 1956).

work here than in Hungary. The Arabs accompany almost all their songs with percussion instruments. The rhythms are often very complicated (the different rhythmic structures arise rather from different ways of accenting similar note-values in the bar). This is the greatest difference between the singing in their country and ours. There are also many primitive melodies (three neighbouring degrees of the scale), and a range outside five notes is infrequent. There are no longer any original stringed instruments (but in their place the violin); their wind instruments use scales peculiar to themselves.

This journey was the outcome of what Bartók had planned in 1906. The theatre of his operations—Biskra—was 200 kilometres from Philippeville. Unfortunately his prophecy that he would manage to live with the heat was not fulfilled, and he had to go home feeling not at all well. However, he wrote an interesting article about his experiences—'The folk-music of the Arabs of Biskra'—for the *Zeitschrift für Musikwissenschaft* (1920). In his article he said that the Arabs possessed a rich culture, the traditions of which were mixed with those of other peoples. For this reason Hungarian folk-song must be regarded as more developed and more artistic than traditional music in Biskra. The influence of Arabian folk-music is also to be felt in a large number of Bartók's works, for instance, in the third movement of the Piano Suite, in the fourth movement of the Dance Suite, and in the 'Arabian folksong' of the 44 Violin Duos.

After returning from Africa Bartók went back once more to the subject nearest his heart—folksong. He knew that the foundation stone of really valuable artistic treatment of folk-song must be the art of the peasants. In order to popularize these ideas, he planned a series of concerts by peasant performers. He was able, however, only partially to carry out this intention. On 18th March 1914 he gave a lecture on the songs and dances of the peasants of Hunyad County. Several peasants were present and performed their own, traditional dances and music.

During the early summer of this year Bartók's young wife also had her first taste of working in the folksong field. On 14th April she wrote to Buşiţia in Belényes:

I am here with my husband for two weeks on an excursion in Maros-Torda . . . and we are both collecting folksongs: my husband spends rather more time on this occasion with the Hungarians, while I go to various Rumanian villages in the neighbourhood of Vásárhely. I am curious to see how successful my first experience of folksong collecting will be. I'm not nervous about taking down the words any more, as I took a thorough course in Rumanian, so that I'm pretty well in practice.

In July, accompanied by his wife, Bartók went to Paris again, and then to Normandy. He then intended to go to the Moldau district and collect songs there. But this was not possible: on 28th July 1914 the First World War started. He wrote in his autobiography: 'The outbreak of war upset me terribly—apart from general considerations of humanity—because it suddenly interrupted almost all my research. There remained only certain parts of Hungary where I could go on working, to a limited degree, up to 1918.' A period in his activity, in the field of his important scientific work, had come to an end.

8 First success

It is of more than symbolic significance that during the First World War Bartók wrote a large number of Rumanian folk-song arrangements. It was no accident that at the very time when chauvinism was at its height he busied himself more than ever with the music of the minorities living in Hungary, and then submitted his work to the public. He hated the war above everything and it was more than fortunate for him that he never had to serve as a soldier. When he learned that Hungary had rushed into a war to protect the interests of other countries he said to his family: 'We shall have to pay dearly for this!'

Every manifestation of war affected Bartók deeply. This, for instance, is from a letter to Buşiţia written on 20th May 1915:

I am thoroughly ashamed that I have for so long neglected to reply to your fine letter of January. In the meantime I also had your letter-card. The reason for my negligence is the depression (which alternates with a certain tendency to let things rip) temporarily caused by the War. The *ceterum censeo* of all my brooding, how-ever, is this; it is all the same to me so long as we remain friends with Rumania. It would pain me terribly if my dear Transylvania were to be devastated, which would also mean that the prospects for completing, or rather for continuing, my work would be seriously impaired.

Unfortunately I cannot anticipate anything good in respect of my position—the future is very dreary!

In the same letter he informed his friend that he was found to be unfit for military service because of general physical weakness (he weighed only 45 kilograms). He continued as follows: 'I even had time for composition, i.e. I was able to compose; it seems that in modern warfare the Muses are not silent. But every day we say: if only all this were at an end. But when will that be?'

Bartók composed a great deal at that time. The *Sonatina on Rumanian folk melodies*, the *Rumanian Folk-dances* (dedicated to Buşiţia), the Piano Suite (Op. 14), the *Rumanian Christmas Songs* and a number of other works that were not published were produced.

The Suite has four movements, of which the first is the only one with the character of a popular folk-dance:

The second movement begins with this theme:

This is a brilliant Scherzo and its high spirits are intensified in the Trio:

The third movement, characterized by a busy drone is, as Bartók himself acknowledged, one of those composed under the influence of Arabian folk-music. The tempo is as fast as it can possibly be:

The last movement, very slow, brings the work to a dignified conclusion:

This kind of expression was frequently used by Bartók as, for instance, in the Second String Quartet, composed not long afterwards.

The Quartet is an important work, which in its original manipulation of material anticipates the later Bartók. One of the mature works of the composer, it dates from his thirty-seventh year. In the opening theme of the first movement,

with its rising fourths, one notices once again the adoption
of a feature of Hungarian folksong:

A second theme, passionate, expressive and melodious, rein-
forces the impression made by the first:

while the third reminds one of Debussy:

The second movement—a Rondo—has inflections reminiscent of the *Allegro Barbaro*, and the interval of the minor
third is prominent.

Because of the prominence of the interval of the fourth the
principal motive of the third movement recalls that of the first,

but the modification of the interval introduces a mood of deep melancholy:

This work belongs to a period when he was under considerable strain.

Now at last came the decisive turn in Bartók's life, which resulted in his first real success. Béla Balázs had published a libretto for a ballet—with the title *The Wooden Prince*—in the progressive journal *Nyugat*. Pressed by Balázs to compose the music for this ballet, Bartók agreed to do so. In the mean time the Director of the Budapest Opera House, Count Miklós Bánffy, had become acquainted with Balázs's text and was unconditionally prepared to give the work a first performance. For the sake of the subject he was prepared to put up with Bartók's music which in his view was ultra-modern. Balázs now urged Bartók to compose the music as quickly as possible, which he did. Bartók himself said:

It probably sounds odd, but I must confess that the fact that my one-act opera *Duke Bluebeard* had been put on one side gave me the impulse for the composition of my ballet. As is well known, *Duke Bluebeard* fell through because of competition at the Opera. The greatest impediment to its performance was that it dealt with the conflict of only two people, and the music was confined to the simple representation of this conflict in abstract form. There was nothing else on the stage. I love my first opera so much that when I had the text of Béla Balázs's piece for dancing I immediately thought that—taking into account the scenery and the bright, richly coloured plot—both works might be performed in one evening. It is superfluous to remark that today the ballet means as much to me as the opera. I began its composition before the War; then came a long interruption, for I had many vicissitudes to pass through.

The story of the ballet is much closer to and much more nearly connected with Hungarian folklore than *Duke Blue-beard's Castle*. Its plot, in brief, is as follows:

> The prince catches sight of a princess and falls in love with her. He would go to her, but at a fairy's command first a forest and then a river are put in his way, so that he cannot approach the princess—who, in fact, does not notice him. The prince has a fresh idea. He dresses up his stick, putting his cloak on it so as to draw the princess's attention to him. He also puts his crown on the stick. But in vain. When, however, he cuts off his hair and puts that on the stick, the princess finally does become aware of him. But it is the puppet and not the man—from whom she turns away in displeasure—that takes her fancy. The fairy animates the puppet, which begins to dance with the princess. Still dancing, they leave the scene. The prince cannot believe his eyes and falls down in despair.
>
> Then the fairy reappears, and at a sign from her the whole of nature pays homage to the prince. Now the princess comes back with the wooden doll, all dishevelled and unsightly. She vainly tries to make it dance once more. She is disgusted with the lifeless puppet; and then she notices the prince. She tries to approach him, but cannot, so that the situation is as at the beginning—but the other way round. The princess humbles herself, and even cuts off her own hair. The prince now looks at the sorrowing princess, and comforts her. The forest, the river and the whole of nature return to their former places.

The Budapest Opera House had a large number of conductors, but there was not one who was willing to undertake the rehearsal of this 'impossible' ballet music. It was a guest conductor, the Italian Egisto Tango, in Budapest at the time, who was enthusiastic enough to say that he was prepared to perform the work. But now the choreographers of the Opera raised difficulties, not seeing how they could rehearse such an 'impossible' piece, in which there was no single traditional element of ballet. At this point Balázs made a bold decision—to rehearse the work himself. Bánffy agreed and immediately gave the necessary instructions; the enthusiasm of Balázs and the eagerness of the dancers solved the problem.

On 22nd February 1917 Bartók wrote to his mother: 'The first and second ballerinas dance merrily to my music. (Are you able to visualize it?)' On 21st March he wrote again:

You are not to abuse Tango. He is the best conductor I have had to deal with up to now. At the time he was not prepared to produce the piece this season only because—as he said—it will need thirty rehearsals, and they also want to produce *Violanta*, Abrányi's opera, and others besides. The 'gracious Lord' (N.B. Bánffy) promised thirty rehearsals. Think of it—thirty rehearsals! Up till now Tango has proved magnificent; because he will not undertake the complete project without being able thoroughly to prepare for it—that's the best thing one can ever hear from a conductor . . . Tango also said that he was very glad that at last he could conduct a Hungarian work, but—he added—he would not have undertaken any other work than mine. When I gave him the score on the Tuesday he said: 'Ik werde eine Woge krank sein von Studium.' (He meant that he would go to work on it with such intensity!) He studied the score for three weeks. (Kerner, for example, doesn't even glance at the score beforehand, and only actually gets to know it at rehearsal.)

Even though the problems of conductor and producer had been solved, however, all difficulties were not yet out of the way. The orchestral players bluntly said that they could not play this unusual music. Friends and acquaintances of Balázs advised him to let the matter drop, to avoid an imminent public scandal. But Balázs would not be put off and was absolutely determined to carry the production of the ballet through.

Bartók realized what was going on. He wrote to his friend Buşiţia on 6th May 1917:

In the last year and a half I have had to go through more bad patches than at any time in my whole life. Take only this world upheaval, which gets worse all the time and—it seems—has ruined my career (I mean my folksong research); for the best areas—that is, Eastern Europe and the Balkans—are completely devastated. This by itself I find crushing. My heart was saddened that the people of the whole of the Fogaras region left their homes with the Rumanian army. Will they ever return, and if so in what circumstances? How I sympathized with the Transylvanian people from Csík and Gyergyó—I used to wander about in these parts. In the end it turns out that it was not in fact the 'enemy' that tormented them, but—and this I would rather not write down—you certainly know who. . . . In such awful conditions I was scarcely able to get the music of a one-act ballet ready for the Opera House. This is a great deal of work even in tranquil times; how much more in this period of distress. And when everything finally was ready troubles intensified; so many unbelievable difficulties, and heated temper because of the Opera House, of which no one can have any idea. What is the Royal Hungarian Opera?! An Augean stable, a dung-hill of beastliness, a home for chaos, the peak of stupidity, where there is but one single man with authority and power to make decisions—even in the tiniest matters—that is, the Government Commissar. . . . This is the last week of rehearsal. Already people are beginning to sharpen their teeth on my account.

In spite of everything Bartók went to the first night on 12th May 1917. What happened was all but a miracle. Tango made possible what had seemed impossible. During the whole of the performance he was all the time correcting the players, on occasion shouting at them; occasionally it seemed as though he would actually jump into the midst of them. The players, who had argued among themselves how to reduce the per-performance to a shambles, gave of their best. When the curtain fell there was a moment or so of complete silence. Then applause came from the gallery, in which the rest of the house joined with great enthusiasm. It showed once again, as Bartók had so often said, that modern music can triumph only when it is well played. On this occasion the convincingly artistic quality of the performance certainly resulted in a victory for modern music, and it was Bartók's first notable success.

The press was favourable. On 13th May the *Budapesti Hirlap* said:

Those who were present at the splendid first night listened eagerly and attentively to the music. They took no exception to its modernity and even enjoyed its interesting novelty. At the end of the piece Béla Bartók was called before the curtain to tumultuous applause. The composer appeared about fifteen times under the spot-lights with his colleagues, Tango and Béla Balázs.

The more the work was repeated the greater its success, so that Bartók and Tango decided to perform *Duke Bluebeard's Castle* during the next season.

The success of *The Wooden Prince* seems also to have aroused some awareness in government circles, for on 2nd December 1917 the following instructions were promulgated by the joint (Austro-Hungarian) Ministry of War:

1. Béla Bartók and Zoltán Kodály, Professors in the Hungarian Academy of Music, as external members of the working body of the Centre for Music History, are directed to edit the Hungarian section of the joint collection of soldiers' songs.
2. The same are to be sent to Vienna for consultations.
3. Béla Bartók is hereby entrusted with the arrangements for the concert planned to take place in Vienna on 12th January, 1918.

Bartók wrote to Buşiţia:

The Ministry for War arranged a large-scale folk-music concert...

in Vienna under the patronage of the King. They tried to get me to take charge of the Hungarian part. As well as Hungarian and Slovak songs (soldiers' songs!) I proposed a group of Rumanian dances. I should be pleased if these were accepted for the programme.

Unfortunately the Ministry would not accept Bartók's suggestion, and so the concert included only military songs from Hungary and Slovakia. In addition to Bartók the following artists took part: Ferenc Székelyhidy the Hungarian tenor; Maria Jeritza; Hans Duhan; Felix Petyrek; the Vienna Male Voice Choral Union, conducted by Bernhard Paumgartner; and Lotte Witt, who spoke the Prologue.

Bartók's connection with Universal Edition, Vienna, began at the time of the 'historical concert'. The following is an extract from another letter to Buşiţia:

The greatest achievement of this year . . . was my success in concluding a contract with a first-class publisher. Universal Edition (Vienna) made me an acceptable proposition in January. After a good deal of negotiation we have finally come to agreement on all points, and in the last day or two I have signed the contract, according to which all my works which are so far unpublished and those still to be written will be published in the next few years.

This is a big thing, because, thanks to our native publishing houses, nothing of mine has been published for about six years, and because a foreign person has never before, perhaps, taken an interest in a Hungarian composer. . . . In any case this contract is so far my greatest success as a composer.

Bartók was quite clear about the meaning of this contract. When he was talking to someone shortly after its preparation he said that he had sold himself 'body and soul' to the firm.

In the mean time a year had passed since the successful first performance of *The Wooden Prince*. Tango did not relax his efforts until he was able to put *Duke Bluebeard's Castle* into the Opera House prospectus. When the first performance took place, on 24th May 1918, the press for the most part took a favourable view. This is what Bartók himself had to say:

The notices of *Bluebeard* were better than those of *The Wooden Prince*. Really, with the exception of *Pesti Hirlap* and *Ujság*, they were all for the work; particularly the two German papers, *Neue Pester Journal* and *Pester Lloyd*.

Dr Izor Béldi, the critic of *Pesti Hirlap*, again spoke frankly about the 'return journey' that he wished the composer to make, 'to the shrine of musical beauty'.

Bartók found that his teaching duties at the Academy became more and more burdensome. Having struggled towards a final fusion of his own style with the elements of peasant song, he wished more than anything else to be able to devote himself to his folk-music researches. He asked the Director of the Academy, therefore, for some reduction in his teaching hours. His request was granted and he was provisionally transferred to the ethnographical department of the Hungarian National Museum where he could continue his scholarly work undisturbed.

In the mean time the war had come to an end. Fortified by the socialist revolution of October 1917, the industrial workers and the peasants of Hungary succeeded in proclaiming a republic and in 1918 a constitution on the Soviet model was established. Directed by the Communist and Social Democrat parties, this lasted until March 1919 and was responsible for the introduction of a number of revolutionary measures. Even though the dictatorship of the proletariat existed only for a brief half-year the effect on the cultural life of the country was considerable. In the field of music the government expressed support for all progressive efforts, and from this Bartók greatly benefited. Béla Reinitz, who had long admired him and who held a decisive place in musical affairs, was a strong advocate and was helpful to Bartók in every way.

The friendship that grew up between the two at this time endured until Reinitz's death.

The new social order also brought drastic changes to the Academy of Music. On 15th February 1919 Ernő von Dohnányi became Director, with Bartók and Kodály as Deputy Directors. Bartók's chief concern was about the intentions of the new government in respect of his researches into folksong. By 9th June 1919 he was able to write that it was proposed to create a Museum for Music, with a department for folk-music under his direction. It was Bartók's view that one of the most important duties of the new State was to raise the standard of musical education. How right he was is proved by the fact that at the present time tens of thousands of musically talented children in the primary schools enjoy a particularly intensive form of musical education.

We turn now to Bartók's later works, particularly to the last one for the stage, *The Miraculous Mandarin*. This pantomime, of which the plot follows, occupies a most important place in Bartók's life:

> In a seedy suburban room three villains compel a girl to entice men, whom they can then rob and murder. She begins by attracting an ageing cavalier who, however, is thrown out by the villains since there is nothing to be got from him. Next comes a shy youngster. But he too is moneyless and is likewise thrown out. Then a mandarin appears. He is all rigid, and so to help him relax the girl begins to dance. Modest at first, the dance grows ever wilder and more and more unbridled, and at the end the girl falls into the mandarin's lap. Inflamed with love for her he tries to embrace her, but, frightened to death of her ghastly client, she draws back. As he begins to throw himself at her the villains come forward to kill him. They throw him to the ground and try to suffocate

him with cushions. When they believe the mandarin to be dead they leave him. But he gets up again, looking towards the girl with fierce desire. His assailants knock him down once more and one of them apparently kills him with a sword. The mandarin collapses, but gets up yet again to pursue the girl. Next the villains hang him. But the mandarin once more does not die. He looks at the girl with longing and she—an idea coming into her mind—gives a sign to the men. She stops resisting his advances and the two of them embrace. Then the mandarin's wounds begin to bleed and after a short death-agony he expires.

The libretto was written by Menyhért Lengyel during the First World War. Bartók's music is a unique expression of horror, fear and a longing that can even conquer death. It is in fact inexplicable how the scene for this ballet could be set far away in Asia, since in the introduction the hideous din of a large European city is heard. One even hears the horns of motor-cars—represented by trombone tone:

A sense of horror precedes the entry of the mandarin. The wind instruments have a shuddering *vibrato*, the violins and the piano a *glissando*, above a *pianissimo* background. There are brutal woodwind chords to illustrate the inhumanity of the villains of the piece:

The lustfulness of the mandarin, as he chases after the girl, is portrayed in oriental inflections in the violas and cellos:

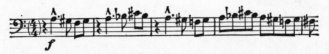

In this work Bartók discusses the problems of humanity with a hitherto unparalleled urgency and passion. In his previous works for the stage he dealt with human love, but in the timeless setting of the fairy-tale. In *The Miraculous Mandarin*, however, the matter is presented in a realistic environment. Love, the emotion that stirs all, here ends in a dance of death. It could not have been otherwise in a world in which a world war could erupt, a war that destroyed culture and all human values. *The Miraculous Mandarin* is the immediate expression of Bartók's urge to protest against war. Nevertheless he also expressed his sense of optimism, in that —in the middle of a warring world, in a time of death and destruction—love, absolutely indestructible, was seen to be the prime force.

The first performance of *The Miraculous Mandarin* did not take place in Hungary until the end of 1945, when—as has already been mentioned—the scene was laid in a romantic, Asiatic setting. This clearly was a watering down of the real idea of the work. Today it is presented, in Budapest, in the more or less contemporary setting that was intended in the first place. Bartók himself had doubted whether the work would ever reach the stage. Attempts to produce it were made during his lifetime—for example, on the occasion of his fiftieth birthday, when he was a figure of world renown. But at the last moment its performance was forbidden on account of its 'immoral' nature. Ten years later the ballet was once again prepared for production; this time it was set aside at the request of the clergy. In 1928 the music was performed as a concert piece.

9 Post-war difficulties

In August 1919 the Hungarian communist government was overthrown, through the intervention of foreign powers and counter-revolutionary influences within the country. The conservatives—a combination of the bourgeois and land-owning classes—seized power, which meant that fulfilment of further progressive intentions became impossible. Literature and art were neglected. Endre Ady was dead, and many talented poets and artists had emigrated in order to save at least their lives. Béla Reinitz was one of them.

The effect of the counter-revolution was also felt in the Academy of Music. Dohnányi, Kerpely, Kodály, Waldbauer and several more were suspended. Bartók asked for an extension of his vacation, 'on account of the medical certificate submitted'. His request was granted. On 28th November 1919 he wrote: 'You ask how I am. So far as I am concerned there is nothing particular to say. I am on extended leave until the end of December. When I applied for this extension it was granted with considerable pleasure. Mr Hubay made his ceremonial entry into the hall of the Academy (he probably provided the necessary Entry March himself).' The last sentence refers to the fact that Hubay was, so to speak, the 'court composer' to the new regime. His official installation as Director of the Academy of Music took place on 21st November 1919.

Disciplinary measures were taken against all those teachers who had expressed any views during the period of the com-

munist government. So, on 23rd October 1919: 'The proceedings against Zoltán Kodály and the rest have not yet started,
and the affair drags on and on. It is obvious that the whole
thing is a comedy. Naturally they are on full pay, but not
allowed to work; so they are better off than the professors
who are not subject to these proceedings.' Bartók had above
all to be thankful for the great esteem in which he was held
in the international field of music; for this reason the reac-
tionary government did not dare to take any kind of action
against him. This is clear from another part of the letter of 23rd
October 1919: 'Nothing unpleasant has happened to me.
Nobody persecutes me (not because there are are no sort of
grounds for so doing—nobody bothers about that—but
simply because no one dares to try anything of the kind).' On
the contrary, the regime tried to do everything to win Bartók
over in order to capitalize on his international reputation. As
the following instance shows, however, he had no intention
of allowing his name to be misused.

In its edition of 20th February 1920 the newspaper *Szózat*
announced the formation of a new Council of Music. Hubay
was to be president, and other members were to include
Szendy (vice-president), Bartók, Béla Szabados, Kerner,
Buttykay and Kern (secretary). The competence of the
Council was to extend over the whole field of music. Immediately after the appearance of this report Bartók made a
statement to the paper, in which he said that he knew nothing
about it and that he had no intention of serving on any commission from which the best musicians in the country were
missing (by which he meant Kodály and Dohnányi). His
statement, however, was not published. In its place was a
larger article, narrowly nationalistic in tone, by Dr Elemér
Sereghy, with the caption, 'Béla Bartók in the service of
Walachian [1] "Culture"'. It mentioned that Bartók had pub-

[1] A Rumanian territory known as the Walachei.

lished an article in a German newspaper on the Rumanian musical dialect in Hunyad County, and the writer went on to complain of his lack of Hungarian patriotism.

The *Nemzeti Ujság* continued a campaign of calumny and on 23rd May Sereghy published another article, 'Concerning Béla Bartók as Hungarian', in which he wrote:

What in time of order and peace may be regarded simply as a consequence of scholarly research and interest can in an extraordinary and critical period be stigmatized as subversive. Why must Bartók publish his article about the culture of the Walachians in a 'foreign' newspaper just now? Why can he not communicate something to foreign journals about his researches in Hungarian folksong, in order to point out the characteristics of our wonderful heritage of folksong which were also recognized by foreigners (Haydn, Beethoven, Brahms)? The Hungarian Government did not subsidize Bartók nor give him leave of absence so that he could work in the field of Walachian music at Hungarian expense. This action, whether it was intentional or unintentional, is in fact an effective way to gain popularity in the eyes of the Walachians.

Bartók did nothing in the face of these attacks. His silence, however, seemed to arouse the papers even more, for their hostility increased. Eventually Jenő Hubay, Bartók's superior, issued a statement as Director of the Academy of Music, which was published on 25th May 1920 in the *Szózat*:

I must at the outset state that for a long time I have enjoyed an excellent relationship, indeed a friendship, with Béla Bartók, and that I consider his talents as outstanding. . . . But this cannot prevent me from saying in the interests of truth that I consider the publication of his article on Walachian folk-music in a German newspaper to be exceedingly ill-timed. At the present time, when we must fight for the maintenance of our integrity to the last drop of our blood, I cannot regard it as other than culpable for us to be in any way concerned with the culture of our minorities.

Bartók always showed a particular sympathy for Walachian

tunes, a considerable number of which he mistakenly incorporated in his collections of Hungarian folksongs. . . . In Bucharest people will now spread it about that Transylvania is an exclusively Walachian musical region. . . . These questions must not today be judged from a scholarly point of view, but only from that of the national interest of Hungary, which at the present time is, in any event, more important than details of scholarship to which in general no great significance can be ascribed.

It was appearently Hubay's statement that first prompted Bartók to issue an energetic refutation not only of Hubay's observations but also of the other attacks. On 26th May his answer appeared in the same journal. He had demanded that, in accordance with the laws concerning the press, it should be published:

I was surprised to read in today's issue of *Szózat* that Principal Hubay endorsed the accusations in the *Nemzeti Ujság*. This now compels me too to go before the public, to draw attention to the most blatant of examples of ignorance, of ill-will and of tendentious errors, in the accusations. I have, indeed, little hope that I can achieve anything with argument, for it is clear that my assailants are completely out of touch with the basic principles of research in musical folklore (for example, they cannot understand that the study of Hungarian folksong makes the study of the folksong of neighbouring peoples essential), and it is also clear that my assailants have no use for scholarly argument but only for personal attacks. The authentic Hungarian original of the article that is the basis of attack was presented by me in the form of a lecture at a meeting of the Hungarian Ethnographical Society as early as February 1914 and was published in the journal *Ethnographia* (1914, pp. 108–15). In answer to the charge that the publication of this article is 'exceedingly ill-timed and most unfortunate at present' I would say that I hold a quite contrary view, because it makes clear the cultural superiority of Hungary. . . . The publication of the article was also desirable so that people abroad could note how much we value our national minorities, how much we care for their cultures, and that they are in no way oppressed. Or does it, perhaps, further the interest of Hungary not to weaken the charges of our enemies concerning the oppression of our minorities? Or, perhaps, do the facts not go some way to refute the allegation that a Royal Hungarian Professor in the Hungarian National Museum as well as collecting folksong material from Hungarians collects it also from among the minorities? My work over several years has made me better qualified, I should have thought, to deal with 'errors' than Professor Hubay, who I know to be quite uninformed about my Hungarian and other collections, in which he has never been interested. If the Professor would sustain his contentions, let him say which melodies I have falsified, or which melodies he considers Walachian, and then let him prove that these are in fact Walachian.

The question is asked: 'Why have I produced no studies of Hungarian folksong?' But there is a mistake here. I have already written about 'The melodies of the Hungarian soldiers' songs' ('Historical Concert, 11th January, 1918', Vienna, Universal Edition) in German and for foreigners. Who is unpatriotic? The man who for more than a decade has spared no pains in researching into Hungarian folk-music, or the one, perhaps, who takes this work for granted with indifference, or is even vindictive and ready with false accusations? Finally I ask this: Is it not the man who, from ignorance, ill-will or mistaken opinion ventures, on the grounds of an article which defends Hungarian interests, to lay a charge of lack of patriotism, who is guilty of malicious misrepresentation?

Yours faithfully,
Béla Bartók.

After all this unpleasantness it is understandable that Bartók again felt the impulse to settle abroad. He had previously written to his mother on 23rd October 1919:

I have already made enquiries in three countries about the possibilities of earning a livelihood. One can indeed live here, but it will not be possible to work here—that is, as I wish (in folksong research)—for ten years. In a word, if I am successful in getting such a job abroad, there is no point in staying here. But if one cannot live on this abroad it is better, for example, to teach in Vienna rather than in Budapest. There at least are good musical institutions (orchestra, opera, etc.), whereas here everything is on the brink of ruin, since the best men—the only men, Tango, Dohnányi, etc.— have been thrown out.

The three countries in which Bartók had made inquiries were Austria, Germany and Transylvania. But he did not in fact emigrate.

In the meantime a change in the direction of the Budapest Opera had taken place. Radnai was the new Director, and the question was again raised as to whether one of Bartók's works for the stage might not be performed. It seemed, however, impossible. Bartók insisted that the names of the librettists should be printed on the play-bills, which was disallowed by higher authority since Béla Balázs and Menyhért Lengyel had both emigrated after the downfall of the communist government. It was only when Balázs had given his consent that Bartók was prepared to remove the librettist's name from the programme in order to have *The Wooden Prince* performed. The ballet was duly prepared, but the Opera House would not pay royalties to the librettist. Bartók made representations to the authorities and, in Balázs's name, said that he would ensure by law that the claims of an author living abroad were settled. As a result the Director, for better or worse, was obliged to pay the money due to Balázs.

A noteworthy composition for piano came from the year 1920—the Improvisations, Op. 20. The work should be entitled 'Variations on Hungarian peasant songs', but in so far as the technique of variation form and also melody are concerned it relates more to Western European music than to Hungarian folk-music. In no work did Bartók ever again depart so far from the Hungarian folk tradition. In this respect this composition symbolizes his struggle towards a definitive, personal style, but one still based on the songs of the peasantry. This struggle led in the first place to an early crisis of extreme severity, which, however, was soon overcome through Bartók's singleness of purpose.

The Sonatas for violin and piano are also relatively distant from the characteristics of folksong. In construction they are similar to the Piano Sonata, the First Piano Concerto and the Third and Fourth String Quartets of 1926. The elements of classical form are wholly absent, and one has the impression that they are improvised fantasias. Bartók himself had something to say about the sonatas dedicated to Jelly Arányi, a friend of his youth, who was living in London as a violin virtuoso. He wrote as follows in a letter to his concert agent Romulus Orchias on 4th October 1924: 'The violin part of the two violin sonatas . . . is extraordinarily difficult, and it is really only a violinist of the top class who has any chance of learning them in such a short time. I would recommend the second sonata, since this is considerably shorter and somewhat easier than the first.' With these two works a stage of Bartók's creative career came to an end. The period of research and experiment was followed by one in which the idioms of Hungarian folksong were effectively incorporated into his own style.

At the beginning of the twenties his activity as composer was somewhat diminished: at this time he was pursuing his researches into folksong more vigorously and preparing his fundamental book on the subject.

On 25th March 1921 he was forty years old. In his native land the occasion was passed over in silence, but in Vienna a whole issue of the *Musikblätter des Anbruch* was dedicated to him. His autobiography also appeared in this journal. It may have been approximately at this time that a young man with whom he was acquainted said to him that he would like to become a virtuoso pianist. Bartók answered: 'Look here! I have not heard you play and am therefore unbiased. I can only say to you: be a lawyer, and if you have any talent also go in for composition; the pianist, even if he has the greatest gifts, does no more than a wood-cutter's job until he succeeds in becoming a professor in the Academy of Music.' These words allow a deep insight into Bartók's experiences during his earlier career as a pianist, and explain things which, ever sparing in the use of words, he never spoke of.

In 1922 he visited England, Wales, France, Germany, and Italy, during his six weeks' vacation. Most important to him, however, was his visit to Transylvania, where he gave six concerts. In London he gave the first performance of his first Violin Sonata with Jelly Arányi.[1] The most important critics, among whom were Edward J. Dent, Cecil Gray and Philip Heseltine, noticed his concerts, his piano-playing and his works. Unfortunately he did not have the opportunity to meet the leading English composers. He did hear a piece by Eugène Goossens, but said later that it was nothing special, only well-constructed routine stuff. While in London he heard Violet Gordon Woodhouse (1872–1968), English harpsichordist, play works by Bach, Scarlatti and Couperin. She also played some old English dances which he particularly liked. At Aberystwyth, in the middle of March, Bartók, introduced by Walford Davies, played pieces of his own and a Beethoven trio with members of the University staff.

In Paris he met Stravinsky, whose works had made a great impression on him, for the first time. He was not able, however, to get on friendly terms with the man. Stravinsky preached that music should be entirely objective, and that the composer therefore should exclude all emotion from his works. Bartók could not accept this thesis and his own work was in complete contradiction to Stravinsky's principles.

---

[1] Bartók gave two concerts in London, the first, a private one, being arranged by the Hungarian Chargé d'Affaires. The sonata was played at the second, public, concert.

When in Paris he also gave a recital in the Théâtre du Vieux Columbier arranged by *La Revue musicale*, which gave him the opportunity to meet Henry Prunières (1886–1942), who introduced Karol Szymanowski (1882–1937) to him.

The noteworthy part of his German tour was his stay in Frankfurt, where *Duke Bluebeard's Castle* and *The Wooden Prince* were performed. Their success was limited, but in August 1922 Bartók's first Sonata for Violin and Piano was played at an International Music Festival in Salzburg. As a result of the interest created by the festival those taking part decided to form an International Society of Contemporary Music. The prime mover was Edward Dent and the first festival of the new society took place in Salzburg in 1923: Bartók was represented in the programme with his second Violin Sonata. Similar festivals took place in succeeding years and Bartók's works were regularly included. In 1925 he was represented in Prague by the Dance Suite (see p. 121); in 1927, in Frankfurt, by the first Piano Concerto; in 1933, in Amsterdam, by the second Piano Concerto; in 1934, in Florence, by the variations from one of his Rhapsodies for violin and orchestra; in 1936, in Barcelona, by the Fifth String Quartet; and in 1938, in London, by the Sonata for two Pianos and Percussion.

Bartók benefited greatly, both spiritually and materially, from his tour of Western Europe in 1922. He was particularly successful with his concerts in Britain, from where, as he had written on 16th March, he had hoped 'to be able to bring home a fine lot of money'. When he returned home he found many troublesome matters awaiting him, and there were all kinds of business to be dealt with. The question of his mother's nationality was one thing that was to cause him worry. But there were other things threatening to take his life off course. On 13th August 1923 he wrote to his mother about his personal problems, which were concerned with his impending divorce and projected second marriage. We know that he had a probing, combative nature, and that he had no liking for the easy way. Márta Ziegler, on the other hand, was always submissive, unconditionally accommodating herself to her husband, in whom she saw a great genius. It was perhaps precisely this submissiveness that got on Bartók's nerves in the long run. On the other hand, it certainly was no easy task to be the wife of a genius.

The break came about in the following way. It was possibly in the summer of 1921 that a young girl turned up in the Academy of Music to play some piano pieces to Arnold Székely, a colleague of Bartók. She wanted to study the piano and to become a pianist. Székely formed a good opinion of the girl—her playing of Liszt especially impressed him—and at once told Bartók about this talented newcomer and asked him if he would take her on. After examining and approving her, Bartók said that he was prepared to accept her as his pupil. Her name was Ditta Pásztory and in due course she became Bartók's second wife. She had a passion for the composer, as all his other girl pupils did, but for a long time she had no idea that he was interested in her other than as a talented artist. Márta was actually responsible for Bartók's decision, since she urged him to seek a divorce and to marry again. After the split she remained in contact with him, often visiting him to see her son Béla. Once Bartók had made up his mind about Ditta Pásztory he produced a new masterpiece, as he had done when he got engaged to Márta. This we know as the Dance Suite, although it is in fact a third Suite for Orchestra.

Since 1912, because *The Miraculous Mandarin* had been such a great disappointment, Bartók had not composed anything for orchestra. But now an opportunity came his way which made him renounce his intention not to write such music. For the Jubilee of the union of Buda and Pest as the capital city the Hungarian Government decreed a celebration of which the climax should be a Festival Concert. Dohnányi's *Festival Overture*, Kodály's *Psalmus Hungaricus* and a new work by Bartók were to be given their first performance.

The Dance Suite, therefore, was a commissioned work, but it none the less represented an important milestone in Bartók's development. The opening of the first movement is strikingly original:

The rhythm is the main substance of this theme and in a series of variations it is illuminated from many sides by different instrumental combinations. This movement ends gently, after which there is a *ritornello*:

which, slightly varied, is repeated, to bind together the individual movements.

The theme of the second movement, *Allegro molto*, is that of a lively dance, and so also is that of the following movement:

Over the fourth movement Bartók wrote *Molto tranquillo* and here there is a melancholy theme:

After which the Finale—an *Allegro* movement of violent energy—follows, with:

Strongly percussive throughout, impetuous and uninhibited, the Finale brings the whole work to a joyful conclusion. On 10th January 1931 Bartók sent Octavian Beu a letter which tells us what he thought of the themes of the Dance Suite: 'No. 1 is partly, No. 4 is wholly oriental (Arabian) in character; the *ritornello* and No. 2 are Magyar; while in No. 3 Hungarian, Rumanian and even Arab influences are intermingled. The theme of No. 5, however, is so primitive, that one can only say that it is of a primitive peasant character and one must refrain from giving it a national classification.'

The Dance Suite shows the great advance made by Bartók since his Four Pieces for orchestra. The manner in which themes are blended into an organic whole, and the last movement, are evidence that by now he had arrived at true mastery in his treatment of the orchestra.

119

The following three years provided another pause in his career as composer. Such silence in the case of great composers always signifies a period of artistic ripening. So far as this was concerned Bartók was no exception. These years served as preparation for a new period of creativity, one of great master-pieces. But he needed this respite in order to delete a sense of guilt that pressed on his conscience: he assembled all the results of his folksong researches and in 1924 published his epoch-making book, *Hungarian Folksong*. The preparations for this book reached back to 1920; and when he was busy on the first Violin Sonata the fundamental principles of this musicological work were already determined. Now it was time to put everything into definitive form. Immediately after its publication the book compelled attention all over the musical world, was translated into several languages, and was considered generally by musical scholars as the foundation for research into all kinds of folksong.

A particular feature of Bartók's scholarly work is its meticulous adherence to facts, and its total omission of abstract speculation. Nevertheless it is extremely original and suggestive. The conclusions expressed in his book have, virtually without exception, stood the test of time and are still tenable today. *Hungarian Folksong* is an internationally important work not only on account of its incomparably rich content, but also because it represented a declaration of war on the cultural policies of the Horthy régime. It showed beyond doubt and in the most convincing and scholarly man-ner that the true folksongs of Hungary were not in the least degree similar to those which were paraded by the rulers of the country. From morning till night these unauthentic 'folk-songs' were heard on the radio—and were naturally accepted abroad as authentic.

The fruits of Bartók's labours during the three years in which he as good as gave up composition altogether comprised these contributions to scholarship: *The Folk-music of the Rumanians of Maramures*,[1] *Folksongs of the Hungarians of Transylvania* (with Kodály) and essays on folk-music instruments and biographies of Hungarian composers (excepting Liszt) for the *Dictionary of Modern Music and Musicians* published in London in 1924. The only music written during this period was the song cycle, *Village Scenes*, a set of five Slovak songs arranged for female voice and piano.

In 1924 and 1925 Bartók made several recital tours abroad, of which the one to Italy was the most important. He reported to Buşiţia on 17th March 1925: 'I had a series of four recitals in Italy, which took me as far as Palermo. In a place like this it is a pleasure to perform and worth all the trouble ... The audience was enthusiastic, and they will have me here in Palermo again next year.' At the International Festival in Prague in 1925 the audience became acquainted with Bartók's masterpiece, the Dance Suite. The extraordinary success of the work ensured that before long it was known throughout Europe. The Prague paper *Bohemia* had this to say:

After all the problematic pieces that predominated on this occasion this was real, full-blooded music. It typifies the thoroughbred individuality of this composer, who has so fundamentally revolutionized the music of his native land. He has freed it from those external influences which were conspicuous until now and has given it a new look. Bartók gives us no more syncopated pieces in the *Czardas* manner nor over-sentimentalized tunes: he has gone back to the original sources of Hungarian folksong and dance, and has re-created them in a manner of his own. A kind of music, of barbaric power in its rhythms and ebullient temperament, that carries itself along with urgent excitement, has emerged. The impression given by this Suite—Bartók's most significant creation for orchestra—was of something elemental. No work by any of

[1] *Sammelbände für vergleichende Musikwissenschaft*, iv.

the other foreign composers present was given such a tumultuous reception, and Bartók had to take call after call.

Other composers who produced works at this Festival included Janáček, Satie, Milhaud, Malipiero, Novák, Martinů, Křenek, Busoni, Stravinsky, Vaughan Williams and György Kósa. The latter, a pupil of Bartók for piano and Kodály for composition, was commended by Paul Stefan for his 'considerable impressionistic talent and knowledge of instrumentation'. Kósa's contribution to the Festival was his *Six Orchestral Pieces*.

The interpretation of Bartók's Dance Suite in Budapest had left much to be desired—a reason for its indifferent reception there. But before long the people of Budapest were able to hear a model performance, since in November 1925 the Prague Philharmonic, conducted by Vaclav Talich (1883–1961), came to the city on tour and included the Dance Suite in their programme. In *Népszava* there was a remarkable notice by Sándor Jemnitz, who laid special emphasis on the fact that the whole work, from beginning to end, had to be repeated. The following represents the general tone of the notice:

The Budapest public was utterly astonished, for no one was perpared for so much beauty, so much that was so bewitching in content and form. Who could have imagined this scorching, electrifying, shattering, and at the same time thrilling magic, after that memorable first performance, with its suggestion of war's alarms? The Budapest public became aware of one very simple fact this Thursday evening. It solved the riddle of Columbus's egg and understood that this 'damned ultra-modern music' was beautiful —if properly played. We have been so inoculated with the works of Bach, Mozart and Beethoven, that without making mistakes we cannot determine what must be attributed to a false conception or interpretation. When a piece is heard for the first time the creative and interpretative factors are combined. It is only a practised ear that can distinguish between the two at a first hearing—and only then if it has retained its capacity for imagination.

The Dance Suite and its striking success in Budapest were for Bartók a starting-point for a series of compositions which can be regarded as his most mature works.

10 Years of fulfilment

After his three years of respite from composition Bartók came before the public in 1926 with a work bearing witness to the maturity that he had achieved during this period. The work was the Piano Sonata. With this representative composition Bartók turned again to the classical tradition, within the limits of which, however, he had something quite new and impressive to say.

The Piano Sonata makes great demands on the performer, requiring considerable keyboard skill. In this work the piano plays the role of a percussion instrument, and even the middle, slow movement lacks the usual lyrical quality. Without doubt, up to this point this is Bartók's most important work for piano, and it is more than a pity that it is his only Piano Sonata.

The first movement immediately shows that it is built on rhythmic elements, beginning with a percussive motive that is subsequently worked through the movement. A certain similarity with the melodic style of the Dance Suite is unmistakable:

The second movement also begins with a strong percussive gesture:

This movement too is of a fundamentally rhythmic character; with its mood of depression it forms a contrast with the first. The third movement, with this pentatonic theme, has a highly national character:

The next work was the cycle of pieces for piano, *Out of Doors*, of which the most interesting and valuable item is 'Night Sounds'—dedicated to Ditta Pásztory. This work aims at expressing all the feelings and impressions which are awakened in the human imagination by the stillness of woods and fields at night. This involves a quite unique form of expression which the composer presents in the very first bar:

The completion of the first Piano Concerto was another high point of 1926. Based on the simplest material—one speaks of motives rather than of themes—this work is, nevertheless, in no way primitive but unprecedentedly complex. The fact that the piano here too takes on the nature of a percussion instrument is obvious, and for long stretches percussion provides the only accompaniment.

Important elements in Bartók's style came as a result of his turning back to the Baroque. In a letter to Edwin von der Nüll he wrote: 'In my youth my ideal of beauty was not so much the art of Bach or Mozart as that of Beethoven. Recently the situation has somewhat changed, for in the last few years I have concerned myself a good deal with pre-Bach music, and I believe there are traces of this to be detected in, for example, the Piano Concerto and in the nine new little piano pieces.' His interest in the contrapuntal style of Bach and his predecessors can in fact be precisely demonstrated in works of this period.

In 1927 only two important works—the Three Rondos and the Third String Quartet—appeared. The former, based on themes from the songs of the minorities living in Hungary, are very rewarding pieces for pianists. The Quartet was dedicated to the Philadelphia Music Society, which had organized the competition at which it received the first prize of 6,000 dollars.

Ten years had passed since Bartók had written his last Quartet. It is not surprising, therefore, that in the new work there are no traces of the subjective lyrical feeling and romantic expression that were so conspicuous in the Second Quartet. The whole of the Third Quartet is strongly marked by imitative techniques which Bartók had not previously used with such consistency. The principles of variation are used with equal consistency and this gives the entire quartet the stamp of organic unity. The whole work is crowned by a fugue based on previously heard themes and parts of themes. The subject at once appears familiar to the listener since there has been considerable preparation for it:

Towards the end of the year Bartók paid his first visit to the U.S.A. His first concert took place in Carnegie Hall, New York, on 22nd December 1927 with the Philharmonic Orchestra, conducted by Willem Mengelberg. In place of the First Piano Concerto, which he had originally chosen, he played his Rhapsody (Op. 1). In the same month he gave a recital, organized by the Pro Musica Society, with his fellow countryman József Szigeti in the Gallo Theatre. The programme consisted almost entirely of his own works. This visit to the U.S.A. was relatively strenuous, with a move to a new centre every four or five days. Philadelphia, San Francisco, Los Angeles, Portland, Seattle, Denver, Kansas City and Cincinnati were some of the cities on his itinerary.

Unfortunately the success of the tour bore no relation to the strain which it imposed. Audiences expected something completely modern, out-of-the-way and sensational, and the snobs among them were disappointed. The rest simply did not understand Bartók's music. In a letter written in January 1928 he made these general observations on his impressions of the United States for the benefit of his mother:

It is very interesting to come here once, but now I have had enough.

Generally speaking, continually travelling here and there was not all that tiring—one actually only becomes indolent as a result of 'inactivity'. Sitting all day long in a railway train, sitting in a hotel, waiting to leave, waiting for the beginning of a concert: all this gives one little inclination to productive work. After several weeks of producing nothing one has had enough of it.

In the same letter he had this to say of the American way of life: '[People] ... keep up with the times, but sometimes they are only successful in doing so with difficulty. There are so many new cities here, and the cultural movement is just starting. . . . This country is so vast and yet so uniform!' Bartók's preference for anything unusual or exotic comes out in another part of the same letter:

I arrived in San Francisco at 8 o'clock at night and straightway went to a Chinese theatre. . . . This was certainly the most interesting thing that I saw in this country. I stayed there till midnight, and wanted very much to remain till the end, but that wasn't possible. Except for myself and a man in the ticket office there were no white people at all in the theatre.

After his return Bartók said in conversation that he had not enjoyed the U.S.A., that everything there was conducted on an arid commercial level. This, because of his nature, was disagreeable to him, and he could not bring himself to resolve to live in that country for a longer period.

In March 1928 the First Piano Concerto was performed by the Budapest Philharmonic. There were excellent notices in the press; the following excerpt is from the *Pesti Napló*:

The more lucid and classical Bartók becomes, the more complex and individualistic he is. And the more complex he is in his pellucid classicism the more elemental, 'barbaric', and 'Asiatic' he becomes ... But who can express through the inadequacies of words all those gigantic revelations of poetic power that are to be perceived in this wonderful music. It is certain that the Piano Concerto (particularly the first two movements) is the greatest work that Bartók has written.

In this year Bartók composed his two Rhapsodies, which actually go back somewhat to the so-called 'folklorist' style. These two works, especially the first, might almost be said to be in a style aimed at the public. But in Bartók's hands this style also acquires distinction and validity. The first Rhapsody has enjoyed great success, not only in its original form for violin and piano, but in many different arrangements.

After his American tour Bartók wrote his Fourth String Quartet which was dedicated to the Pro Arte Quartet. An interesting point about the composition of this work is that the ensemble was already rehearsing the first movement before the fifth (and last) was completed. During rehearsal Bartók withdrew to a corner of the room, where the last part of the final movement was quickly written down. (The movement must have been in his head long before and the end merely needed 'copying'.)

The quartet is extremely interesting, particularly in respect of design, for it shows Bartók's 'arch' form at its clearest and most pronounced up to that time. That is to say, the individual movements—in themselves variations—are symmetrically grouped around a stable centre. For example, the fifth movement is a variation on the first, and the fourth on the second. The centre-point is the third movement. These relationships may be shown diagrammatically:

Within the course of Bartók's works the Fourth Quartet has an important place, since it opened up new possibilities of expression that were further exploited in his later works.

In the second half of 1928 he was invited to undertake a tour in the Soviet Union, where his music was naturally by no means unknown. In fact the Society for Modern Music had arranged an exhibition in which works by Schoenberg, Hindemith, Ravel, Falla and Bartók were displayed. The Soviet journals had always paid attention to Bartók, and Professor Bjeljajew, one of the more distinguished musical scholars, had written with considerable discernment on the character of the piano works, finding connections between Bartók's *Allegro Barbaro* and many works by Prokofiev.

Bartók travelled to Russia at the beginning of 1929 and gave performances in several places, including Moscow, Leningrad, Khar'kov and Odessa. He received much encouragement and took away a variety of impressions of the Soviet Union, and it was a source of satisfaction to him that he could play his music to its citizens. He was particularly impressed by the kind of people who constituted the concert-going public. Here were people who not only listened to serious music enthusiastically but also invested it with a particular significance. It was not, as in some other countries, a case of a privileged section of the community claiming for itself the right to enjoy and to understand music. Bartók always used to say that up to this time he had never been greeted so enthusiastically as in the Soviet Union. When he had returned from this journey, somewhat exhausted, the *Pesti Napló* wrote:

Béla Bartók came back completely worn out. During his Russian tour he caught several colds. He was in a fever when he returned to Pest, but now the fever has subsided and he complains mainly of feeling weak.

His first concert, which was very successful, was in Moscow. Erzsi Paulay appeared at the second concert with her husband, the Italian Ambassador. Bartók then performed in Leningrad, Khar'kov, Odessa and the larger towns of the Ukraine. When he was about to leave for home it was suggested that he should return to Russia in the following year. But since he had to perform in America he could give no definite answer.

On 20th March 1929 the historic concert, at which the Fourth String Quartet received its first performance, took place in Budapest. The audience also heard another new work —*Twenty Hungarian Folksongs*, several of which were most successfully introduced by Mária Basilides, with Bartók as accompanist. This song-cycle is substantially different from his previous compositions, especially those which are arrangements of folksongs. It is, perhaps, most nearly related to *Village Scenes*. The piano accompaniment has here achieved independence, which was not previously the case in Bartók's songs. This independence derived less from studying Bach than from the music of the old Italian and Netherlands masters of the pre-Bach era. *Ostinato* passages, pedal points and various highly individual details alternate with sections reminding us of the *Improvisations*. There are also to be found here examples of the recasting of particular folk melodies—as, for example, in 'The shepherds' song' (No. 4).

We now turn to Bartók's greatest work for chorus and orchestra, the *Cantata Profana*, based on an old Rumanian folk-ballad. On 10th January 1931 Bartók wrote to Octavian Beu:

It is only the text of the *Cantata Profana* that is Rumanian. The thematic material is my own composition; it is not in the remotest degree similar to Rumanian folksong, and in several sections there is nothing in a folksong style. This work, therefore, must be described as a 'Setting of the text of a Rumanian *Colinda*'.[1]

---

[1] The *Colinda* is a purely secular Christmas song.

The subject of the cantata is summarized by the composer as follows:

An old man had nine sons, whom he trained for nothing but hunting. When they were grown up they went hunting in wild country, until they came to a mysterious bridge. They crossed this bridge and were changed into stags. Their father prepared to look for them, and having followed their track and found them begged them to come home to their grieving mother. His sons, transformed into stags, answered: '. . . our slender bodies—do not want to wear clothes—nestle only in green leaves—with light tread—will run only on the woodland moss—our mouths will drink no more from your full cups—only from the clear spring.'

The style of the work is highly individual, even unique. At the beginning chords are piled one on top of the other in the orchestra. The double chorus ('Hear the tale of a marvel') produces something quite remarkable; the two alto parts sustain G♯ and F♯, above which the sopranos lift a melody which, with its perfect fourths, is unmistakably Hungarian:

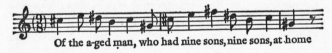

Of the a-ged man, who had nine sons, nine sons, at home

Next comes the description of the hunt, first in the orchestra:

and then in the chorus, in an extended fugue of enormous energy based on this theme:

The fugue, with its many outbursts and interjections, is turbulent. Chords are piled on one another like granite rocks, describing the hunt and the discovery of the miraculous bridge. After the furious dissonances a unison passage is heard:

This recalls an old Székely folk-ballad, which is also a miraculous fairy-tale. The father discovers his transfigured sons in the forest and addresses them thus:

But the eldest son, his favourite, answers:

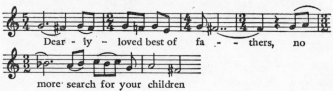

This is a mild, even an ingratiating, melody, but it develops with threatening defiance:

Ah! all falls in dire ru-in.

The sons are already at one with nature, and can never again go back:

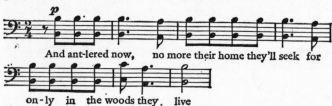

And ant-lered now, no more their home they'll seek for

on-ly in the woods they live

The *Cantata Profana* is, without doubt, the finest hymn to the union of man with nature in contemporary music; at the same time it heralds a new view of mankind, and of music, that becomes more and more obvious in Bartók's later works. It expresses the longing of men for freedom and for a life worth living, as no other work of Bartók does. It is to be considered not only from a technical, musical angle, therefore, but also in relation to aesthetics and psychology. It is a remarkable piece of self-confession—a view confirmed by the fact that Bartók wrote the text himself.

We now turn to two other important works, which appeared in 1931: the Second Piano Concerto and *44 Duos for two violins*. The Piano Concerto once again shows Bartók's 'arch' form, already noticed in the Fourth Quartet. The first theme is so characteristic

that it is easily recognizable in the varied form in which it reappears in the third movement. The second theme

shows a leaning towards the Baroque, while the third, in the slow second movement, is really a chorale melody, in spite of its dissonant harmony:

In the middle section there are the humming effects, with which Bartók always depicted nature; above all there is the tranquillity for which man yearns after all his struggles and cares.

This is the central part of the whole work. After the humming the chorale melody returns. In the third movement the second theme of the first movement reappears, though in slightly altered form:

and the second theme of this movement, a variant of the

corresponding theme in the first movement, is already familiar:

In this work the percussion instruments are again given a prominent role, and it is not surprising—since this was the case in previous works—that the piano also serves as one of them. A more important characteristic is the clash of opposite forces culminating in a relentless battle characteristic of Bartók both as a composer and as a scholar.

The *44 Duos* have a similar purpose to the four volumes of *Pieces for Children* for piano. Neither work is very difficult and both can be played by the young. But whereas the piano pieces come from the beginning of Bartók's development as a composer, those for the violin belong to his maturity. The former opened up a new world of sonorities, the latter bear witness to a masterly technique of part-writing. In spite of the two-part nature of the pieces, Bartók manages in some of them to impress the technique with characteristics of national music. For example, in No. 8—*Slovak Song*—we notice how the second violin performs its accompanying function with a constant rhythmical figure:

8. Slovak Song

In complete contrast to this is the way in which the second violin maintains its independence in No. 14, a Hungarian melody:

14. Cushion Dance

As a third example we take No. 26, *Satirical Song*, also of Hungarian origin, which is presented in canon:

26. Satirical Song

On 4th March 1931 Bartók once again visited Pressburg. On this occasion he gave a lecture on the influence of folk-music on composition in general. His stay in the city was the occasion for a celebration, for the Toldy Society with which he had close personal connections (István László Németh, its chairman and conductor, had been a pupil of his) was re-named the 'Béla Bartók Choral Union'. There was a further honour for him this year: his nomination to the League of Nations Commission for Intellectual Co-operation. He was the only musician belonging to this body. He had much of interest to say about his impressions of the first conference in Geneva in a letter to his mother dated 13th July 1931: 'Thomas Mann spoke several times, always in German, and was clever and interesting.' Although he hated all kinds of ceremony and formality, Bartók was not bothered this time, 'since I could talk with congenial people . . . I also spoke to Thomas Mann a good deal'. He also described a lunch given by the Hungarian Ambassador: 'The lunch was not agreeable; apart from the hideous croaking of Mme. X [1] these smooth, sophisticated diplomats are after all an entirely different breed . . . from artists.'

From Geneva Bartók travelled to the Mondsee in Austria, where he was to teach at a summer school for Austrian and American musicians. Other members of the teaching staff were Paul Pisk, Paul Weingarten (who, however, having learned that no students had enrolled for him, left at once), Theodor Lierhammer (a Polish singer), the Róth String Quartet and Josef and Rosina Lhévinne. The greater part of those who were announced to come did not appear. Of the eight students assigned to Bartók only one was present on the first day; another two came later. But since he had been paid he carried on teaching.

On 25th March 1931 Bartók celebrated his fiftieth birthday. There were those in Hungary who wished to arrange a special celebration in honour of the occasion, and at the Opera House a production of *The Miraculous Mandarin* was prepared. But in order to carry out the intention it was desirable that the scenario, which had been so much criticized, should be fundamentally altered, so as to make it 'presentable'. Bartók would not agree to this, stating that since the music had been composed with a particular story in mind nothing could be altered without damage to the whole work. As a result, the performance did not take place, and Bartók was never to see his last work for the stage given in Hungary.

After this Bartók devoted himself once more to his folk-song researches, the conclusions of which were published in *Our Folk-music and the Folk-music of Neighbouring Peoples* (1934). Starting from a renewed definition of its particular character, Bartók examined in this work the influences extending from and into Hungarian folksong. First, he divided such influences into four categories: (1) exact take-over,

[1] Mrs Wilson, widow of the President of the United States.

(2) take-over with minor alterations (e.g. extension of material, slight distortions), (3) take-over with significant changes, (4) take-over of alien structures and rhythmic figures.

Direct influences from German folksong were slight; indirect influences came by way of the songs of the Bohemian-Moravian region. Rather more frequent were interrelations, particularly those between Hungarian and Slovak folksong. At the time of the oldest Hungarian song Slovak influence was very strong, much more so than the other way. In all other cases of contact with folksongs of other countries Hungarian folksong was always the stronger and consequently took root in alien soil. The reason for this, Bartók determined, was its lively character and taut rhythms.

It followed that the melodic repertory of the Hungarian village had a character entirely its own, and that the neighbouring peoples for the most part took over only those songs which were similar to their own, which they did not alter. A brief quotation from this work shows Bartók's objectives: 'I would have published the results of my researches even if they had turned out less favourable. I was all the more delighted to arrive at a conclusion which is more favourable than could have been imagined. It is possible that in the future my conclusions may be modified in some details. But I have the firm belief that I have not made significant errors.'

In 1935 Bartók gave to the world his Fifth String Quartet, which was written during August and the first few days of September. It was completed on 6th September, and the first performance was given in Washington, D.C., in April 1935 by the Kolisch Quartet (Rudolph Kolisch, Felix Kuhner, Jenő Lehner, Benar Heifetz). This work is also in 'arch' form, the first movement and the fifth, and the second and the fourth, being thematically related. It is strongly contrapuntal throughout—some of it is in canon—and is among the composer's most complex works.

The opening is strongly reminiscent of the songs of lament of the Székely people:

The *Scherzo* is marked *Alla bulgarese*, with each bar dividing with 4+2+3 quavers.

In spite of this the movement is not Bulgarian, though it has the general quality of folksong. In the fifth and last movement there is a striking passage. After the complexities of the movement have created a climax the first episode occurs. This is not only simple, but decidedly primitive, and accompanied by an Alberti-bass figure:

Doubtless there is a satirical intention, which is also suggested by the instruction *meccanico*, but precisely what Bartók intended to express has been the subject of much speculation. My own view is that this passage is designed to confound those who found Bartók's music 'too difficult' and wanted him to write something 'easier'.

In 1934 Bartók was awarded the Knight's Cross, *Meritul Cultura*, First Class, by the Rumanian Government, which gave him much pleasure. What gave him even more satisfaction, however, was that after 28th August he was released from teaching the piano at the Academy of Music in Budapest, so that as a member of the Hungarian Academy of Sciences he was able to go on with his researches into folksong. He now worked in this field with Kodály. The great collection of Hungarian folksong that was the result of their labours could not, however, be published till long after Bartók's death, and after the liberation of Hungary.

In 1935 Bartók completed a series of choral pieces for equal voices, about which Kodály wrote: 'From 1925 onwards I often suggested that he should write choral music. For a long time he did not do so, but some time later—a dozen years or so—came out with a whole bundle. At that time he started looking at the music of Palestrina, which made a deep impression on him. It is a matter for permanent regret that he could not pursue this further.' [1]

Some of the items from the choral cycle were given their first performance at a concert on 7th May 1937, at which Bartók played some of the pieces from *Mikrokosmos*. He had something to say about this concert in a letter which he wrote to Mrs Müller-Widmann on 24th May 1937:

At the concert on 7th May I really played some of the *Mikrokosmos* pieces. However it was not these but the pieces for children's choir which were the most important part of the concert. It was a great experience for me to be able to hear my little pieces from the lips of

[1] Zoltán Kodály, 'Bela Bartók the Man', 1947.

those children at rehearsal. I will never forget how fresh and cheerful their voices sounded. The voices of these children—particularly children from the suburban schools—sound so natural, and remind me of the sound of our still unspoilt folksong.

Bartók not only wanted to educate the children of the suburban working class; he also thought of the adults and lent his support to their efforts to come to terms with worthwhile music. Together with Kodály he took part in the work of the Association of Hungarian Workers' Choirs. A piece for male-voice choir, *Elmult időkből* ('From the Past'), belongs to this period. This work is in three movements, and on the first page is inscribed, 'Based on the texts of old songs and folksongs'. A kind of coda to the *Cantata Profana* and expressing the same philosophy, it is extremely difficult and only to be performed by a really good choir.

On 18th May Bartók was elected a Corresponding Member of the Hungarian Academy of Science. He gave his inaugural address in 1936; it was published later under the title, *Liszt-problemák* ('Liszt Problems').

On 1st January 1936 the Budapest newspapers printed a report under the caption, 'Bartók refuses the Greguss Prize'. This prize was founded by Ágost Greguss (1825–82), a celebrated Hungarian writer, in the 1880s. Six prizes, one of them for music, were to be given out of the interest on the endowment, but as a result of inflation and devaluation, a Greguss Prize had come to have little more than honorific value. The award, marked by the presentation of a medal, was made every five years. Bartók refused the prize, and the *Pesti Napló* reported:

To check the accuracy of this report we approached Béla Bartók, who made the following statement:

'The report is true: I am not accepting the Memorial Medal. I have written to the Kisfaludy Society [1] today to inform them. One reason for this refusal is that the bestowal of the Medal is based on an error, for my *First Suite for Orchestra does not belong to the period* 1929–34. The first complete performance of my Suite was in 1909, when it was conducted by Jenó Hubay. . . . Thus my Suite could not be considered. The second reason for refusal is that *in the years 1929–34 many more mature compositions than the First Suite were performed.* I do indeed love this youthful work, *but in my judgement better works than my composition have certainly been performed in the last six years.*

'According to this any other old work could be brought before the Committee. Either the Greguss Prize follows the rules or it does not . . . In my letter which I sent to the Kisfaludy Society I wrote that *they might choose another adviser, since anyone incapable of judging the externals of a musical work was hardly likely to be able to evaluate its intrinsic value.*'

Doubtless the award of the Greguss Prize on that occasion took place under very particular conditions. Those who were responsible wished to demonstrate their condemnation of Bartók's manner of composition and to show that they considered his artistic career subsequent to the First Suite for Orchestra as misguided. But the way in which Bartók refused this 'recognition' not only made clear to the public what lay behind the intention but provided an energetic reply to those who would have liked to hinder progress.

On 27th January 1937 Bartók's most recent work—*Music for Strings, Percussion and Celesta*, written to mark the tenth year of the Basel Philharmonic Orchestra—was given its first performance in Basel under the direction of Paul Sacher. This is perhaps the most organically developed work of Bartók on the lines we have already observed in the Fourth and Fifth Quartets. The themes of every movement come from

[1] Greguss had been the secretary of this society. (See *Kisfaludy*, Appendix C, p. 201.)

the fugal theme of the first. And each separate movement is so spontaneous, so passionate, so immediate in experience that it is as if Bartók had written the whole work down in one impulse and not, in fact, worked it out with great ingenuity. The scoring is for two string orchestras, celesta, harp, piano, xylophone, cymbals and other percussion—a combination which naturally offered a number of possibilities to the composer. A point deserving special notice is the layout of the orchestra, with the percussion between the two string groups.

The first movement is a fugue on the theme:

(An octave lower in the original)·

There is no countersubject. The exposition, though basically strict, is unusual in one respect: the even-numbered entries start progressively a fifth higher (E, B, F♯, etc.), the odd-numbered entries a fifth lower (D, G, C, etc.). When the most distant tonality, of E♭, is reached the succeeding entries show the theme and the order inverted, until the tonality of the opening recurs. After this comes a coda. The tremendous concentration of this movement is caused by the way in which it moves towards the tonality of E♭ through a huge *crescendo* taking six and a half minutes—something that never occurred again in Bartók.

The second movement is in sonata form. The principal theme is divided between the two string groups, and has a distant relationship with that of the first movement. Here too the fugal theme appears allusively.

In the third, *Adagio,* movement there is the same kind of atmosphere as in *Night Sounds*—which is more and more to be found in Bartók's works. Fragments of the fugue subject turn up as links in connection with repetitions of the principal theme of the movement:

(An octave lower in the original)

In the fourth and last movement we meet a ravishing theme, of a kind seldom to be met with in Bartók:

The fugue subject again appears, but this time in diatonic rather than in the original chromatic form.

The whole movement is basically in *Lied* form, but each time the main motive occurs it is varied.

In the summer of this year another significant work appeared—the Sonata for Two Pianos and Percussion (composed in July–August 1937). As well as the two pianos, the score includes three cymbals, xylophone, tamtam, two side-drums, two antique cymbals (*crotales*), bass drum and triangle. The first performance was given by Bartók and Ditta Pásztory in Basel on 16th January 1938; the percussionists were Fritz Schiesser and Philip Rühling. (In the event of there being too much for two players to do, Bartók advised that a third could be engaged for the xylophone.) The whole work is intensely rhythmic, while the way in which the tone-colours of the percussion are grouped suggests Asiatic, perhaps Malayan, influence.

After a slow but always impassioned introduction that grows in excitement, the first theme, reminiscent of that of the *Allegro Barbaro*, is stated:

The second theme, following a characteristic interlude, makes a complete contrast with the first:

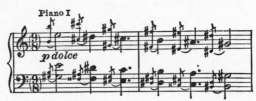

In the development section the three themes (including that of the interlude) are all treated. At no time, however, do they appear in their original state, being varied even in the recapitulation. A long coda, which is in fact a modern fugue on the interlude theme, brings the movement to an end. This movement takes about half the playing time of the whole work. In spite of this the listener feels no disproportion in performance, but hears the complete work as a unified and organic whole.

The second movement is built on two themes. The first is restful in character:

The second theme, on the other hand, grows out of an agitated figure:

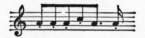

The third and last movement is dance-like, with the main theme given out first by the xylophone:

In this movement it often happens that the percussion instruments carry the main argument of the music, the piano meanwhile sustaining a pedal point. Bartók himself remarked in a

147

letter of 11th November 1937 that there were 'immense difficulties, particularly in the first movement' of this work.

As a result of Bartók's international reputation as a composer and scholar he received an invitation from the Turkish Government in 1936 to assist in the establishment of folksong research. The invitation entailed his giving three lectures on the subject; in addition to this he was to organize two folksong collecting expeditions. It was the last that persuaded him to accept the invitation. Despite all obstacles—he fell ill after his arrival in Turkey—the results of this excursion were good, for he collected ninety Turkish melodies. Unfortunately he was not able to do anything with this material until some years later—during his period in the U.S.A.

The most important composition of this time, without doubt, is the Violin Concerto commissioned by the violinist Zoltán Székely, to whom it was dedicated. At first Bartók inclined to a large-scale work in variation form for violin with orchestral accompaniment, but Székely was insistent that it should follow the 'classical' concerto form. When it was composed, and Székely had approved and accepted it, Bartók confessed to him that he had actually carried out his original plan in that the third movement was a free variation on the first.

The work is written in three-movement 'arch' form. With its succession of fourths the opening theme betrays its Hungarian origin:

The similarity between the beginning of the third movement and that of the first is clear:

The theme of the variations in the middle movement—a pure, somewhat languishing, song—is one of Bartók's most beautiful inspirations:

The Concerto was first performed on 23rd March 1939, in Amsterdam, with the Concertgebouw Orchestra conducted by Mengelberg.

At the same time Bartók also completed his Trio for Violin, Clarinet and Piano (entitled *Contrasts*). The movements of this work brilliantly unite the characteristics of Hungarian *verbunkos* of the nineteenth century with the rhythms and melodic inflections of oriental music. Bartók dedicated this work to Szigeti and Benny Goodman, by whom it was first performed in New York on 9th January 1939, with Endre Petri as pianist. It is the only published chamber music by Bartók to use a wind instrument.

Meanwhile ever darker clouds were assembling on the political horizon of Europe. Already in 1937 Bartók had received from the German Reichs-Musikkammer a questionnaire designed to establish the 'Aryan descent' of composers whose works were played in Germany. This questionnaire was the subject of a letter which Bartók wrote to Mrs Widmann on 13th April 1938. With bitter humour he said that both he and Kodály considered the whole thing illegal and that they would not therefore answer the questions. But, he wrote further, one could have an interesting and amusing time with the answers. One would, for instance, have to declare that one was not an 'Aryan'—it being well known that Hungarians did not belong to the Aryan peoples but to the Finnish-Ugrian language group. One could also give an interesting answer to the question 'When and where were you wounded?' Thus: 'On 11, 12, 13 March 1938' (at the time of the *Anschluss*).

Hitler's entry into Austria was a severe blow for Bartók, who wrote to László Rásonyi on 28th April 1938:

This damned German advance puts me in such a difficult position that I have been worrying about it and brooding over all the questions it brings in its train for weeks. My publisher and also the company that deals with the fees for performances of my music are in Vienna! That means that all my income falls into the hands of robbers—it is doubtful how I can be free from their claws, and if any liberation at all is possible.

He was convinced of Hitler's plans for conquest and was certain that sooner or later Hungary would be brought into line. In Julia Székely's *Béla Bartók, the Scholar* there is information about Bartók's political views. The following excerpt is taken from this book:

Bartók went with me a little way along the street. At the Pest end of the Chain Bridge he stopped to buy some papers. 'Wait a minute,' he said, 'I'll only glance at the news.' He leafed through the papers in his hand quickly and nervously, until he came to the report of the Spanish Civil War. He read several lines and then all at once made an agitated, impatient gesture. 'It is terrible,' he said, 'the Republicans are defeated! Why don't the Communists of other countries send help, with aeroplanes or in some other way?' It was clear that this question very much concerned him.

Bartók also foresaw the threat of war. On 9th October he wrote:

I can hardly see any collaboration between the infamous Axis and the Western countries; the great reckoning must come, but later and under favourable conditions. One must believe that it would be better for this grievous event to take place now. . . . So far as is possible I live a retired life. I have no wish to meet people; every living person is a suspected Nazi. Almost every day I work ten hours exclusively on folk-music material. But I ought to work twenty hours merely in order to make some headway. A painful situation—but I should like so much to finish this work before the impending catastrophe occurs.

11 Farewell to Europe

Under the stress of prevailing circumstances Bartók now had
to consider leaving Hungary for a prolonged period. How
difficult it was for him to come to a final decision may be
seen from his letters, which revolved round the problem of
emigration, but which only gradually began to show that he
regarded it as inevitable and necessary. Thus on 10th January
1939 he wrote to Mrs Zoltán Székely:

Your letter fills us with alarm. Is the situation really as bad as you
see it? Since March we are of course convinced that things will go
from bad to worse so that it will be impossible to work or, in
general, to live here. But would I be able to carry on with my most
important work (I mean my research work) in the country you
mention? I don't believe so. If I can only 'vegetate' there, then
there is no point in changing the 'place of residence'. I think it is
infinitely difficult to come to a decision on this matter, and I am
really at a loss as to what to do. . . . It is surely unpleasant enough
for me to live so near the clutches of the Nazis—which means,
entirely in their clutches; but if I could live elsewhere it wouldn't
be any easier—so it seems at the moment.

On 3rd June 1939 he once more denied harbouring
thoughts of emigration: 'Your news, that I am going to leave
Hungary, is wrong. But it has lately got around, and many
other people speak to me about it.' In the same letter he wrote:

If anyone stays here, in spite of having had the chance of leaving,
people will say that he gave silent consent to all that happened

here. And one cannot contradict this in public, for that would only result in disaster, which would, therefore, make staying here pointless. But people could also say, how tragic is the state of a country where everyone must stay in his place and support what goes on, as is now only possible. The only question now is, if within a reasonable period of time there is hope of being able successfully to help. . . . I have no confidence—but this is entirely an individual matter. . . . In a word I am for the time being entirely at a loss, but I feel I ought to go while the going is still good. I would not wish, however, to influence others in this respect.

In 1939 Bartók completed his great pedagogic work *Mikrokosmos* ('Piano music from the very beginning') which he had begun in 1926. There are seven volumes (153 pieces in all), the first two of which are dedicated to his younger son Péter. *Mikrokosmos* is a vast, comprehensive work which pianists may use from the first to the most advanced grade. There are two aims in the collection. First, the pupil is to achieve a good and musically competent style without the usual unmusical 'exercises', the pernicious influence of which is only too obvious later on. Second, the beginner is to be so acclimatized to modern musical idiom and so well educated that he will always be in contact with contemporary music and be able to recognize in it the characteristics both of progressive and conservative styles. What Bartók himself thought of *Mikrokosmos* we learn from a newspaper article of 3rd October 1940:

One piece in *Mikrokosmos* was originally meant as the tenth of *Nine easy piano pieces* (which appeared as early as 1926). For some reason or other it was taken out. At that time I was already considering the idea of writing piano pieces for elementary instruction. In fact I began work on this project in the summer of 1932.

When the first part of the first volume was ready I had a fine opportunity to give the project a practical test. In 1933 my younger son Péter was insistent that we should let him learn the piano. I came to a bold decision and took over this duty—for me one that was a little unusual. Apart from exercises in singing and technique the child had music only from *Mikrokosmos*. I hope that it was useful to him, but I must say that I myself learnt much from this experiment. . . .

The individual pieces in *Mikrokosmos* are in different forms, beginning with simple eight-bar structures and leading to designs of much greater complexity. The pupil can play the easiest pieces after a month or two. As well as a great variety of rhythms one finds different kinds of counterpoint, from simple pedal point to canon. Many pieces are bitonal, others are pentatonic (based on different tonics), others again are in the church modes. In respect of melody, pedagogic considerations are also to the fore, so that characteristics of the tone-series used are given prominence, and particular intervals emphasized. With three exceptions the 153 pieces in *Mikrokosmos* are based on original melodies composed by Bartók. From time to time, however, one is convinced that one is hearing authentic Slovak or Hungarian folksong—a consequence of Bartók's endeavours to incorporate the folk-music of the various nationalities within his own works.

Comprehensive works with an educational purpose as valuable as *Mikrokosmos* are rare in the history of art. One can, perhaps, best compare it with the works of similar intention by J. S. Bach, which were also the result of practical teaching in a worthy artistic setting. But *Mikrokosmos* is significant in another way, since it gives important advice not only to pianists but also to composers. The student of composition finds in it short solutions—which are very much to the point—of many of the problems of his craft. Here too we may again draw a comparison with Bach, who observed in the preface to his *Inventions* that it was their purpose to teach students 'not only to have good ideas but also to develop them well and, above all, to achieve a *cantabile* style in playing, and at the same time to acquire a taste for composition'.

In spite of the doubts that tormented Bartók at this time composition proceeded apace. On 18th August 1939 he reported to his elder son from Switzerland, where he was then staying:

I must work. To be precise, for Sacher; it is a commission (something for strings); this makes my situation similar to that of the old composers. Fortunately the work went well; it is a piece of about twenty-five minutes' duration and I was ready with it in fifteen days—I finished it exactly yesterday. And now I must fulfil a second commission: a string quartet for Z. Székely (for the New Hungarian Quartet). Since 1934 I have worked almost entirely to commission.

He was here referring to his *Divertimento*, dedicated to the Basel Chamber Orchestra. It is, perhaps, the friendliest, most accessible, work of Bartók's 'classical' period, and can be fully enjoyed at a first hearing by those of lesser musical experience. The principal theme of the first movement is particularly engaging; the sense of the dance is here, and from the very beginning the atmosphere is of a 'Divertimento':

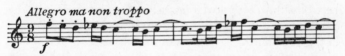

The lyrical middle movement is weighed down by an oppressive feeling that surely reflects Bartók's mood at the time he was writing it. He had heard from home that his mother was seriously ill. The third movement is optimistic, as its theme clearly indicates:

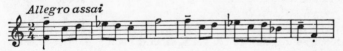

Immediately after the completion of the *Divertimento* Bartók began a new work, the Sixth Quartet—which was to be his last work for this medium. Here we no longer find Bartók's 'arch' form. Instead the unity of the composition is ensured by the use of a 'motto' theme. This appears at the beginning of the quartet in its basic form and in the course of the work it is more and more woven into the texture of development. It is melancholy, even inconsolable, in character:

It was when he was working on this quartet that Bartók heard that his dearly loved mother—who had made so many sacrifices for him—had died. His grief finds outlet particularly in the last (fourth) movement of the quartet.

How much he was affected by his bereavement is shown in a letter which he wrote to Mrs Widmann, in Basel, on 2nd April 1940:

It is now three and a half months since I lost my mother, and all the time it seems as if it happened yesterday. It is difficult to describe my state of mind, it is also, perhaps, difficult for others to grasp—perhaps. But hardest of all to bear are the self-reproaches— that I might have done everything differently to have made my mother's life, and her last years, easier. Now it is too late. There's nothing to be done. It is true that everything was so confused, so complicated, and that recently there were so many conflicting factors coming all at once. For example, take last summer: I went to Saanen so that I could remain there undisturbed and write two works as quickly as possible. I spent three and a half weeks there, and the works were entirely, or partly, finished; but I had taken three and a half weeks away from my mother. I can't make up for this any more. . . . There are many things of that kind in the past, which I can't now do anything about.

With the death of his mother the last thread that had bound him to Hungary was severed, and he decided to leave his native land for a time. This decision is reflected in the Sixth Quartet, which is his Farewell to Europe. Even the less gloomy parts of the work, the Burletta and the caricature of a March, are full of bitterness, and self-torment and melancholy are inescapable in these movements too. The sense of deep sorrow conveyed by the last movement is a farewell not only to his mother but also to Hungary. On 14th July 1940 he wrote to Gyula Kertész:

Because of the way things are now, not only can I write no choral pieces, but, for all practical purposes, nothing new. In all probability this year will vanish in this way. What the future brings only Wotan (and his vice-regent) knows. At the end of September (if possible) I must again go to the U.S.A., but with my wife, for an extended period.

Bartók had to visit the United States again because he had undertaken a recital tour there with Szigeti at the beginning of 1940. So far as Bartók was concerned this tour was the first step towards his extended sojourn in the U.S.A. His American friends and admirers knew of his plans for emigration and where it was possible tried to help him. While he was touring the country Bartók wanted to secure an appointment against the time of his emigration. Jenő Antal, a member of the Roth

Quartet, had suggested getting in touch with Columbia University. Douglas Moore, Paul Henry Láng and George Herzog were also helpful, and so the repeat journey that he wanted to make to the United States with his wife became even more likely. On 17th May 1940 he wrote quite definitely: 'I hope that I shall be able to return to the "free" land in October at latest.' (Bartók himself put the word 'free' in inverted commas.)

The formalities were completed with reasonable speed, and the Bartóks prepared for their great journey. Shortly before their departure Bartók made his will, the last part of which formed his political testament.

In the event of a street being named after me after my death, or of a memorial tablet being erected in this connection in any public place, I direct as follows:

So long as the former Octagon and Rotunda Places in Budapest are named after the same men [Hitler and Mussolini] as now; further, so long as a place or a street in Hungary is named after these men, no one is to name a place or a street or a public building after me; nor is any memorial tablet to me to be erected in a public place.

On 8th October the Bartóks gave a farewell concert in the Academy of Music. The *Esti Kurir* reported on 9th October:

Yesterday evening the Great Hall of the Academy of Music was filled with the leading figures in our cultural life. Hungary took her leave of Béla Bartók and his wife, Ditta Pásztory. The world-famed composer bewitched his audience, and the honour done to both artists came from deep feeling, and passionate enthusiasm. . . .

The concert opened with Bartók playing Bach's Piano Concerto in A major, after which Ditta Pásztory gave the first public performance in our country of Mozart's F major Concerto. Then we heard Mozart's E♭ major Concerto for Two Pianos in the original version prepared by the Bartóks, with which they had been so successful in Paris two years ago. The greatest master of our century played some of the *Mikrokosmos* pieces that had not previously been heard.

In the autumn of 1940 it was no longer easy to undertake a journey abroad, and the Bartóks must have been well aware of the difficulties involved. They had to wait for weeks before they could obtain transit visas for France and Spain. The worst of the difficulties, however, came only after leaving the Spanish frontier. The omnibus to Barcelona broke down, and the Customs examination was very severe. The Bartóks had to leave part of their luggage behind in the hope that it would be sent on to them in Badajoz within three days. There they were informed, however, that they would get the rest of their luggage in Lisbon. In Lisbon they were told that it would be sent to New York as soon as possible. They stayed only a few hours in Lisbon, where they embarked—leaving behind more than 300 kilograms of luggage.

The following passage from his last letter from Europe to Mrs Widmann gives an idea of Bartók's emotional state at the time: 'To say good-bye is difficult, very difficult. And to think that one has seen this lovely country—your country [i.e. Switzerland]—for the last time, and to wonder what the future holds for our friends who are here! But we can do nothing. It is really not a question of "must it be"; because it must be.'

On 29th October 1940, after a voyage of ten days, they arrived in New York harbour.

12 The United States

The Bartóks had scarcely arrived in the United States when they had the chance of appearing before an American audience. Their first concert, at which they played the Sonata for Two Pianos and Percussion, took place in the Town Hall in New York on 3rd November 1940. They gave two more piano recitals later in the month. As in the past, Bartók absolutely refused to teach composition, even though opportunities offered themselves and his material circumstances made it necessary. The Curtis Institute of Music offered him a post that would have required his presence, for composition lessons, one or two days a week, with the rest of his time at his own disposal. But Bartók would not entertain this idea. When anyone tried to persuade him he quietly, politely but firmly said that he did not wish to teach since his own creative work would suffer. On 25th November 1940 he was given an honorary doctorate at Columbia University, and was described in the *New York Times* the following day as a distinguished teacher and master; internationally recognized authority on the folk-music of Hungary, Slovakia, Rumania and Arabia; creator through his composition of a musical style universally acknowledged to be one of the great contributions to the twentieth-century literature of music; a truly outstanding artist who had brought high distinction to the spiritual life of his country.

The Bartóks lived temporarily in Forest Hills, approximately sixteen kilometres from the centre of New York. On

16th December they were delighted when their lost luggage at last caught up with them. Before taking up an assignment at Columbia, they went on tour, visiting St Louis, San Francisco, Seattle, Kansas City and Detroit. In March 1941, on the advice of George Herzog (Assistant Professor of Anthropology at Columbia) Bartók began an analysis of the Parry collection of some 2,500 Jugoslav folksongs. Dr Herzog arranged for Bartók to have his own room in the university where he could devote himself to his work without disturbance. For the time being life seemed bearable. He could work at what he wanted most of all to do; he had no lectures to give nor tutorials to supervise; all he had to do was to continue his research work. There was material available and everything in the way of resources that could have been wished for.

But when his contract with Columbia expired he had to look for other work. Because the prospects of public performance looked anything but brilliant, it seemed that the plan of earning a living in this way was hazardous. At the last moment, however, the university extended its contract and Bartók was able to go on with what he had begun. The result was a scholarly work on Serbo-Croat folksong, published long after Bartók's death, in 1951.[1]

He liked his work at Columbia, where he was graded as a 'Visiting Associate of the Department of Music' and paid at the rate of $3,000 a year. Nevertheless he was always oppressed by a certain insecurity since—as had already happened once —his agreement could be revoked at any time. This feeling of uncertainty naturally weighed on him the more since it was obvious that his stay in the U.S.A. would in all probability be a long one. Nor could he decide fully to adapt himself to the American way of life and to give up his own habits.

[1] Béla Bartók and Albert B. Lord, *Serbo-Croatian Folk Songs* (New York, 1951).

Also his importance, both as a composer and as a scholar, was not properly recognized. Things were made more difficult by the fact that a great many distinguished people were at that time seeking sanctuary and trying to re-establish their careers in the U.S.A. All this had a bad effect on Bartók's health. He was frequently ill, and his wife was constantly having to call the doctor in.

On 8th August 1941 Bartók wrote to Reiner that his affairs were more complicated than they had ever been: 'Things have become so terribly difficult here, and (unnecessarily) complicated ... N.B. I have no lawyer; i.e. I had one, who having messed everything up, left me in the lurch.' On 8th October his business affairs were again disordered: in a letter he bitterly commented that 'everything now depends on the graciousness of the Consul in Montreal'. He was referring to the fact that since up to this time he and his wife had lived in the U.S.A. only as 'guests' they must spend some time 'abroad' (e.g. in Montreal, Canada) and then return to the States in order to regularize the situation.

That he had congenial research work was of small comfort to Bartók when his other living conditions were so joyless and when he had to combat all sorts of troubles. He wrote to Wilhelmine Creel on 17th October 1941 to tell her of his difficulties: 'If I tell you that we have for this season one orchestral engagement, three two-piano recitals, four minor engagements (piano solo or lecture) and that is all, then you easily see how precarious our situation is.'[1]

The future brought nothing better. Bartók wrote again to Mrs Creel on 2nd March 1942:

Our situation is getting daily worse and worse. All I can say is that never in my life since I earn my livelihood (that is from my 20th year) have I been in such a dreadful situation as I will be probably

[1] Original English text.

very soon.... I am rather pessimistic, I lost all confidence in people, in countries, in everything. Unfortunately, I know much better the circumstances [*sic*], than Ditta does, so probably I am right in being pessimistic.[1]

Later in the year, on 31st December, he wrote to say that he had been invited to give some lectures at Harvard University:

This gives us a respite until next fall (no possibilities with concertizing or lecturing; we have a 'unique' engagement in Jan. with the New York Philh. Society, but this is a 'family' business, the engagement was made through my friend Fritz Reiner who is guest conductor in some of these concerts). So we are living from half-year to half-year. ... My career as a composer is as much as finished: the quasi boycott of my works by the leading orchestras continues; no performances either of old work[s] or new ones. It is a shame—not for me of course.[1]

There was one occasion of pleasure to set against all this depression; on 20th April 1942 Bartók met his younger son Péter, by chance, in the subway at 231st Street in the Bronx. The boy had left Budapest before the previous Christmas. His parents had had no idea when to expect him, as the censor had deleted the name of the ship from the cable which he had sent from Lisbon.

On 21st January 1943 the Bartóks again played at a concert, at which the orchestral transcription of the Sonata for Two Pianos and Percussion was performed. This event, which was to be Bartók's last public appearance, was undertaken by the New York Philharmonic Society, conducted by Fritz Reiner.

Bartók was a victim of leukaemia, an incurable disease. The first symptoms of the illness showed themselves in April 1942. At this time he had influenza, which left behind a permanent fever. In 1943 his condition worsened, and after

[1] Original English text.

the concert mentioned above he was so weak that he could scarcely move, his temperature all the time being 4 degrees above normal. The lectures that he had to deliver in order to live completely wore him out. The doctors had no idea of the nature of his complaint, and from May the pain in his joints was so great that he could hardly move at all. In the summer of this year ASCAP (American Society for Composers, Authors, and Publishers) paid for him to convalesce at Saranac Lake (New York State). Here he began to write a new work, a major orchestral piece commissioned before his departure by the Koussevitzky Foundation. What he did not know was that this commission had been given at the suggestion of Szigeti and Reiner. This had to be kept from him, for if he had suspected any hint of charity, he would have refused the commission, which was worth $1,000 to him.

In the beautiful, romantic, wild scenery about Lake Saranac his attacks of fever became less severe, and less frequent, and in the autumn of 1943 the score of the new work, the Concerto for Orchestra, was completed. Apart from the satire in the second and fourth movements the mood of the work is heroic and grand. The conclusion is optimistic, full of the acceptance of life. The title suggests that in the course of the work individual instruments and groups are used as in a concerto.

The opening of the work pictures the Hungarian countryside, with a pentatonic theme which shows a close similarity to the introductory bars of *Duke Bluebeard's Castle*:

Andante non troppo·

In the second movement (*Giuoco delle coppie*) the instruments enter in pairs, always in sixths, as for example at the passage where the bassoons come in after an eight-bar drum solo:

In the course of this movement the consistent use of the same interval is caricatured by the trumpets:

The first bars of the elegiac third movement recall the opening of the first:

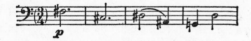

After this there is a somewhat bitter, satirical episode, a kind of comic Dance of Death. The initial theme, tearful but grotesque, extends the emotional range of the whole work:

The last movement, heroic and triumphant, crowns the whole. It is, no doubt, not entirely accidental that the theme that runs through it bears a resemblance to the theme of the variations in the last movement of Beethoven's *Eroica*:

This work is additional proof of Bartók's absolute mastery in orchestration: the way in which each instrument is given the chance to demonstrate its characteristic qualities makes it outstanding in contemporary music. The first performance, with Koussevitzky and the Boston Symphony Orchestra, took place on 1st December 1944.

In October 1943 Bartók had been able for the first time to hear his Violin Concerto, which was played in New York by Tossy Spivakovsky. 'The performance,' he wrote, 'was excellent: soloist, conductor, orchestra were first rate (and the composer too!)'. The following month he met Yehudi Menuhin for the first time and was very impressed by his playing at a concert which included Bach's C major Sonata and Bartók's First Violin Sonata. He wrote to Mrs Creel: 'My sonata . . . was excellently done. When there is a real great artist, then the composer's advice and help is not necessary, the performer finds his way quite well, alone. It is altogether a happy thing that a young artist is interested in contemporary works which draw no public, and likes them, and—performs them *comme il faut*.' [1]

Since Bartók's health showed no signs of improvement ASCAP sent him to Asheville, North Carolina, where he recovered at least a little. In the mornings he would go for long walks and with typical thoroughness study the songs of the birds. He soon had a whole collection of jottings of bird melodies, the most attractive of which he introduced into his next work, the Third Piano Concerto: in the second move-

[1] 17 December 1943. Original English text.

ment he seems to picture the mood of a lonely walker in the woods. His zest for work was re-awakened in Asheville, where he not only composed but also resumed work on his collections of Rumanian and Turkish folksongs. Mostly, however, he concentrated on his Sonata for Solo Violin, the last work that he was to complete.

The first movement of the Sonata is marked *Tempo di Ciaccona*, but this refers only to tempo and not to form, which is, broadly speaking, sonata form. The second movement is a fugue, but much more free than, for example, that by Bach in the G minor Sonata for Solo Violin. It is, perhaps, best defined as a fugal fantasia. The third movement, *Melodia*, shows Bartók's characteristic treatment of variation particularly clearly. The basic principle is that of the *da capo* aria (*ABA*), while the last movement, *Presto*, has a thematic connection with the first. This work requires several hearings before its intrinsic qualities and beauties can be fully appreciated. It was given its first performance by Yehudi Menuhin on 26th November 1944. Bartók was present to acknowledge from the platform the generous applause bestowed on the work. Reviews, however, were unfavourable. They were bound to record the considerable success the work enjoyed with the audience, but this was generally attributed to Menuhin's performance, to which Bartók also paid high tribute.

In February 1944 Péter Bartók reported to the military authorities and was enlisted as a marine. After training he was ordered to Panama. Bartók was against his son becoming a soldier, but Péter wished to acquire American nationality so that he could study in an American university, and so felt he must volunteer for military service. Bartók, however, did not pursue the matter of naturalization for himself any further as he did not wish to stay in the U.S.A. for ever. In the spring of 1945 he learned of the end of the war in Hungary. He was relieved to hear that the Kodálys and the members of his own family had survived the invasion and that his research material was intact. But he was appalled by the destruction and devastation that the country had suffered and felt no desire to return, particularly as the state of his health in any case compelled him to stay where he was. Fortunately his material circumstances seemed to have taken a slight turn for the better. At Christmas 1944 he had been able to tell Mrs Creel that he had had about $1,400 from royalties and performing rights and had also concluded an agreement with Boosey & Hawkes, who were to pay him $1,400 a year, exclusive of royalties and performing rights, for the next three years. This income, even though assured, offered only the prospect of a modest living. It was, however, to be increased by a new agreement for the composition of a string quartet.

There were other commissions as well. William Primrose, the viola-player, suggested that he should write a viola concerto for him. Bartók hesitated for a long time, for he did not feel at all well and did not know in advance if he could maintain his capacity for work. In fact what is now described as his Viola Concerto is not his original creation. After his death he left only sketches for it; in a letter dated 8th September 1945 he reported that it was virtually complete, and that there remained only the task of orchestration. Tibor Serly, one of his friends in America, completed the concerto from the sketches and the first performance of this version was given by Primrose in 1949.

How far Serly's realization matches Bartók's intention we do not know; but in any event this concerto is not to be regarded as an authentic work. The two-piano team of Ethel Bartlett and Rae Robertson also tried to persuade Bartók to write them a concerto. Whether he really intended to compose such a work after completing the Viola Concerto is, at best, uncertain. That he was anxious about his wife's future is, however, certain. He turned, therefore, to the design of a solo concerto, which turned out to be his last work. The Third Piano Concerto, which seems to express the joy of life, was not entirely completed, but all that remained for Serly to do was to orchestrate a few final bars.

The opening bars of this concerto put the listener into a cheerful mood. From the initial humming of the strings:

there emerges a lovely melody for the soloist:

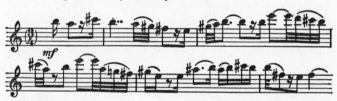

The hum, as of insects, in the orchestra recalls the sounds of nature that Bartók heard in field and woodland when he went walking, and the melody for the piano we may consider as an apotheosis of nature. The same mood is reflected also in the second movement, *Adagio religioso*, a passage for the piano in the style of a chorale:

Religioso is used here by Bartók for the first and only time. It does not mean 'religious' in the ordinary sense of the word but suggests the reverent mood of a man in tune with nature. This union is expressed in the bird songs—memories of those long walks in Asheville—that are to be heard in this movement.

The finale at first bears a slight resemblance to the fifth movement of the Concerto for Orchestra. But in place of the *perpetuum mobile* of that work there is an impetuous dance rhythm:

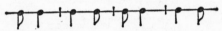

Making much use of this, the piano functions again as a percussion instrument. This movement contains the most varied techniques: thematic metamorphosis, canon and *fugato*. The basic theme, first enunciated by the piano, is reminiscent of Bach, but despite a good deal of Baroque polyphony it does not for one moment cease to be characteristic of the composer:

At the beginning of 1945 Bartók suffered inflammation of the lungs. He got over this, but it was a contributory factor to his death. When he was apparently somewhat better he accepted an invitation, on behalf of his wife and himself, to stay with Menuhin in California. It was arranged with his doctor that this visit should take place in June. In the meantime Péter Bartók was demobilized and came to New York in August 1945. From here he travelled on to his parents at Lake Saranac.

Among the many doctors whom Bartók consulted one of

the most prominent was Israel Rappaport, himself Hungarian born and a native of Budapest. Bartók was already very ill when he consulted Dr Rappaport in 1943, and it was necessary to call in other assistance. According to Rappaport's records those who also had care of Bartók's last years included Dr Nathan Rosenthal, a specialist in diseases of the blood; Dr Salomon Feinman, radiologist and specialist in leukaemia; Professor Emanuel Friedmann, neurologist; Professor Herman Elwyn, ophthalmic surgeon (Bartók also had an eye complaint); and, lastly, the Hungarian-born Dr Frederick Reiss, urologist. The main part of the treatment consisted of blood transfusions and dosages of penicillin. Neither the doctors nor ASCAP spared themselves, in effort or cost, in the endeavour to prolong Bartók's life.

He spent his last days in Mount Sinai Hospital on Fifth Avenue. There at first he had enough energy to look at his collection of Turkish melodies and also to complete his Turkish vocabulary. On 21st September 1945 Tibor Serly visited him. On his bed lay the sketches for the Viola Concerto. He was in great suffering and could scarcely move. Nevertheless he managed to write the last bars of the Third Piano Concerto. Next day his condition so deteriorated that he had to be moved to West Side Hospital.[1] Here decline was rapid, and he lay in a continuous state of coma. On 26th September death released him from his suffering.

Bartók was born in a country of several nationalities, and became a patriot; proud of his Hungarian birthright he strove to bring fame to the land of his fathers, and he remained true to this aim. From the start his patriotism distinguished itself from the narrower kinds, since he was inspired by a true

[1] Then in a block on the corner of Sixth Avenue and 57th Street; it no longer exists.

humanism. The best proof of this is his thorough involvement with the music of the minorities living, often under oppression, in Hungary, as well as with that of small nations in general. To publish the folk-music of the minorities, especially at the time of the First World War, was an act of political criticism, and also of courage.

Hungarian folksong, for Bartók, was not merely a matter of patriotism, but also symbolic of the struggle of the peasantry for recognition. When he went on his research expeditions he saw the people of the countryside not merely as objects for academic scrutiny but as men and women who had their own distinctive contribution to make to the world's culture. Bartók based his own creative work on the foundation of the songs of the peasantry, which in consequence became widely known.

For a long time, most of all in Hungary, he was decried as an 'iconoclast'. People noticed only what was new in his music, without recognizing that it had developed logically from what was traditional. Many of his contemporaries failed to take into account the real basis of his musical style—his concern for the problems of the day. He wrote to Octavian Beu on 10th January 1931: 'The essential idea—of which I became fully aware after I discovered myself as a composer —is: the brotherhood of man, a brotherhood despite war and strife. In so far as I am able I try to serve this ideal in my music.'

At this distance of time it is easy to forget that he lived through the most agonizing period of European history. It is easy to forget that his music was the result of the conflicts that engulfed him and all around him. On 24th May 1937 he wrote: 'Originally we wanted to go to Italy (the Dolomites), but my hatred for Italy has lately grown so intense that I simply cannot bring myself to set foot in that land.'

And again on 24th October 1938: 'One must get away

from here, from the proximity of that pestilential country [Germany]; far, far away— But where? To Greenland, to the Cape, to Tierra del Fuego, to Fiji, or God knows where.'

Bartók left Hungary unwillingly. Had he not done so—so Zoltán Kodály said—his outspokenness would have led to his suppression, possibly to his martyrdom. But his voice could not be silenced. All that he had to say was contained in his music.

Appendix A   Calendar

(Figures in brackets denote the age at which the person mentioned died)

YEAR	AGE	LIFE	CONTEMPORARY MUSICIANS
1881		Béla Bartók, son of Principal of Agricultural College, born March 25, at Nagyszentmiklós, Hungary.	Mussorgsky (42) dies, March 28; Ábrányi aged 59; Agházy 26; Albéniz 21; d'Albert 17; Arensky 20; Balakirev 45; Bantock 14; Bloch 1; Boito 39; Borodin 47; Brahms 48; Bridge 2; Bruckner 57; Bruneau 24; Busoni 15; Caplet 2; Chabrier 40; Charpentier 21; Chausson 26; Cui 46; Debussy 19; Delibes 45; Dohnányi 5; Dukas 16; Duparc 33; Dvořák 40; Elgar 24; F. Erkel 71; Falla 5; Fauré 36; Franck 59; Gade 64; Glazunov 16; Goldmark 51; Gounod 63; Granados 14; Grieg 38; Grovlez 2; Heller 66; Holst 7; Humperdinck 27; d'Indy 30; Inghelbrecht 1; Koessler 28; Lalo 58; Leoncavallo 23; Liadov 26; Liszt 78; Loeffler 20; Macdowell 20; Mahler 21; Martucci 25; Mascagni 18; Massenet 39; Miaskovsky

YEAR	AGE	LIFE	CONTEMPORARY MUSICIANS
			born April 20; Mihalovich 39; Novák 11; Parry 33; Pedrell 40; Pizzetti 1; Pfitzner 12; Pierné 18; Ponchielli 47; Puccini 23; Raff 59; Rakhmaninov 8; Reger 8; Rimsky-Korsakov 37; Roger-Ducasse 6; Ropartz 17; Roussel 12; Rubinstein 52; Saint-Saëns 46; Satie 15; Schoenberg 7; Scott 2; Sgambati 38; Sibelius 16; Skriabin 9; Smetana 57; Stanford 29; Strauss (R.) 17; Suk 7; Sullivan 39; Szabó 33; Taneiev 25; Tchaikovsky 41; Vassilyenko 9; Vaughan Williams 9; Verdi 68; Volkmann 66; Wagner 68; Wolf 21; Wolf-Ferrari 5.
1882	1		Kodály born, Dec. 16; Malipiero born, March 18; Raff (60) dies, June 24–25; Stravinsky born, June 17; Turina born, Dec. 9; Vycpálek born, Feb. 23.
1883	2	Begins to show interest in mother's piano playing.	Bax born, Nov. 6; Berners born, Sept. 18; Casella born, July 25; Szymanowski born, Sept. 21; Wagner (69) dies, Feb. 13; Webern born, Dec. 3.
1884	3	Opening of Opera House in Budapest.	Van Dieren born, Dec. 27; Rózycki born, Nov. 6; Smetana (60) dies, May 12.

Bartók

YEAR	AGE	LIFE	CONTEMPORARY MUSICIANS
1885	4	Erzsébet (Elsa) Bartók (sister) born June 11.	Berg born, Feb. 7; Varèse born, Dec. 22; Weiner born, April 16; Wellesz born, Oct. 21.
1886	5	First piano lessons.	Dupré born, May 3; Kaminski born, July 4; Liszt (74) dies, May 10; Ponchielli dies, Jan. 16; Schoeck born, Sept. 1.
1887	6		Atterberg born, Dec. 12; Borodin (53) dies, Feb. 27; Valen born, Aug. 25; Vomáčka born, June 28.
1888	7	Béla Bartók sen. (33) dies Aug. 4. Béla jun. at school in Nagyszentmiklós and then Nagyszőllős.	Durey born, May 27; Heller (73) dies, Jan. 14.
1889	8		Shaporin born, Nov. 8.
1890	9	First compositions.	Franck (68) dies, Nov. 8; Gade (73) dies, Dec. 21; Gál born, Aug. 5; Gurney born, Aug. 28; Ibert born, Aug. 15; Martin born, Sept. 15; Martinů born, Dec. 8; Salazar born, Mar. 6.
1891	10	Programme piano piece on the Danube's course.	Bliss born, Aug. 2; Delibes (55) dies, Jan. 16; Finke born, Oct. 22; Jirák born, Jan. 28; Prokofiev born, April 23.
1892	11	Debut as pianist and composer in charity concert in Nagyszőllős.	Franz (77) dies, Oct. 24; Honegger born, March 10; Howells born, Oct. 17;

YEAR	AGE	LIFE	CONTEMPORARY MUSICIANS
			Kilpinen born, Feb. 4; Lalo (69) dies, April 22; Milhaud born, Sept. 4; Wood (Thomas) born, Nov. 28.
1893	12	Grammar school in Pressburg, lessons with László Erkel, attempt to supplement family income by giving piano lessons.	Absil born, Oct. 23; Goossens born, May 26; Gounod (75) dies, Oct. 18; Hába born, June 21; Mompou born, April 16; Tchaikovsky (53) dies, Nov. 6.
1894	13	Period of schooling in Beszterce, necessitated by mother's duties as teacher, before resettlement in Pressburg.	Chabrier (53) dies, Sept. 13; Dessau born, Dec. 19; Moeran born, Dec. 31; Pijper born, Sept. 8; Piston born, Jan. 20; Rubinstein (63) dies, Nov. 20; Wagenaar born, July 18; Warlock born, Oct. 30.
1895	14	Wins the Eötvös prize.	Castelnuovo-Tedesco born, April 3; Hindemith born, Nov. 16; Jacob born, July 5; Orff born, July 10; Sowerby born, May 1.
1896	15	National millenial celebrations.	Ádám born, Dec. 13; Bruckner (72) dies, Oct. 11; Gerhard born, Sept. 25; Hanson born, Oct. 28; Sessions born, Dec. 28; Thomson (Virgil) born, Nov. 25; Weinberger born, Jan. 8.
1897	16	B. plays at school concerts, making an impact by his performance of Liszt; numerous pieces	Brahms (63) dies, April 3; Cowell born, March 11; Korngold born, May 29; Tansman born, June 12.

177

YEAR	AGE	LIFE	CONTEMPORARY MUSICIANS
		composed of which a few (for piano) have survived.	
1898	17	Jubilee of War of Independence; B. plays pseudo-folksongs at school concert in keeping with general nationalistic mood.	Eisler born, July 6; Gershwin born, Sept. 25; Rieti born, Jan. 28.
1899	18	Enters Academy of Music in Budapest after refusal of place in Vienna; seriously ill.	Auric born, Feb. 15; Chausson (44) dies, June 10; Jemnitz born, Aug. 9; Poulenc born, Jan. 7; Tcherepnin (A.) born, Jan. 20.
1900	19	First appearance as pianist at Academy concert, March 31. Seriously ill again in summer.	Antheil born, July 9; Burkhard born, April 17; Bush born, Dec. 22; Copland born, Nov. 14; Křenek born, Aug. 23; Sullivan dies, Nov. 22; Weill born, March 2.
1901	20	Promise of B.'s playing at Liszt memorial concert.	Egk born, May 17; Finzi born, July 14; Pepping born, Sept. 12; Rheinberger (62) dies, Nov. 25; Rubbra born, May 23; Verdi (87) dies, Jan. 27.
1902	21	Discovery of an enthusiasm for music of R. Strauss; publication of settings of 4 poems by Lajos Pósa.	Szábo born, Dec. 27; Walton born, March 29.
1903	22	Diploma; plays piano in Vienna, Nagyszentmiklós, Berlin.	Berkeley born, May 12; Blacher born, Jan. 3; Kadosa born, Sept. 6; Khachaturian

YEAR	AGE	LIFE	CONTEMPORARY MUSICIANS
			born, June 6; Wagner-Régeny born, Aug. 28; Wolf dies, Feb. 22.
1904	23	*Kossuth* Symphony scandalizes Austrians in Budapest, but praised in Manchester; completes Rhapsody for Piano (Op. 1).	Dallapiccola born, Feb. 3; Dvořák (62) dies, May 1; Kabalevsky born, Dec. 30; Petrassi born, July 16.
1905	24	Failure in Rubinstein Competition in Paris; beginning of friendship with Kodály and folksong research; first Suite for Orchestra (Op. 3).	Blitzstein born, March 2; Farkas born, Dec. 15; Jolivet born, Aug. 8; Lambert born, Aug. 23; Meyer born, Dec. 8; Rawsthorne born, May 2; Tippett born, Jan 2.
1906	25	20 folksong arrangements (with Kodály) issued; tour of Spain and Portugal with Ferenc Vecsey.	Arensky (44) dies, Feb. 25; Frankel born, Jan. 31; Lutyens born, July 9; Shostakovich born, Sept. 25.
1907	26	Succeeds Thomán as professor in Academy of Music; second Suite for Orchestra (Op. 4); folksong excursion with Pál Bodon.	Fortner born, Oct. 12; Grieg (64) dies, Sept. 4; Maconchy born, March 19; Ránki born, Oct. 30; Veress born, Sept. 1.
1908	27	Kodály appointed professor; B. publishes piano pieces, completes Violin Concerto for Stefi Geyer, and works at first string quartet; visits France.	Distler born, June 24; Macdowell (46) dies, Jan. 23; Messaien born, Dec. 10; Rimsky-Korsakov (64) dies, June 21.

YEAR	AGE	LIFE	CONTEMPORARY MUSICIANS
1909	28	Marriage with Márta Ziegler; peformance of second Suite in Berlin and first Suite in Budapest.	Albéniz (48) dies, May 18; Murrill born, May 11; Martucci (53) dies, June 1.
1910	29	*Two Portraits* (Op. 5) for orchestra; music by B. and Kodály played by Waldbauer Quartet and introduced by Béla Balázs; birth of son, Béla; Debussy visits Budapest.	Balakirev (73) dies, May 29; Barber born, March 9; Reinecke (85) dies, March 10.
1911	30	Foundation but quick demise of New Hungarian Music Society; *Duke Bluebeard's Castle* (Op. 11) completed.	Mahler (50) dies, May 18; Menotti born, July 7.
1912	31	Bartók - Reschofsky *Piano Method*; Norwegian visit with Márta Bartók.	Coleridge-Taylor (37) dies, Sept. 1; Massenet (70) dies, Aug. 13; Szervanszky born, Jan. 1.
1913	32	Journey to North Africa to collect folkmusic.	Britten born, Nov. 22; Dello Joio born, Jan. 24.
1914	33	Visit to France; outbreak of First World War.	Liadov (59) dies, Aug. 28; Sgambati (73) dies, Dec. 14.
1915	34	Period of retreat and intense concentration on composition.	Goldmark (84) dies, Jan. 2; Skriabin (43) dies, April 27; Searle born, Aug. 26; Taneiev (58) dies, June 19.
1916	35		Blomdahl born, Oct. 19; Butterworth (31) dies, Aug.

YEAR	AGE	LIFE	CONTEMPORARY MUSICIANS
			5; Granados (48) dies, March 24.
1917	36	Première of *The Wooden Prince*, Budapest, May 12; B. and Kodály required to edit 'soldiers' songs' by Austro - Hungarian War Ministry.	
1918	37	Participation in 'Historical Concert', Vienna, in aid of war widows and orphans; Contract with Universal Edition (Vienna); *Duke Bluebeard's Castle* peformed in Budapest, May 24; revolutionary government in Hungary.	Bernstein born, Aug. 25; Boito (76) dies, June 10; Cui (83) dies, March 24; Debussy (55) dies, March 25; Parry (70) dies, Oct. 7.
1919	38	Counter-revolutionary government makes difficulties for intellectuals and bids for B.'s support without success.	Leoncavallo (61) dies, Aug. 9; Vlad born, Dec. 29.
1920	39	Refusal to serve on new government Council of Music on grounds of conscience; attacks on B.'s scholarly conclusions; thoughts of emigration.	Bruch (82) dies, Oct. 2; Fricker born, Sept. 5; Járdányi born, Jan. 30.
1921	40	Issue of Viennese musi-	Humperdinck (67) dies, Sept.

181

YEAR	AGE	LIFE	CONTEMPORARY MUSICIANS
		cal journal devoted to B.; Ditta Pásztory becomes a pupil.	27; Saint-Saëns (86) dies, Dec. 16; Séverac (47) dies, March 24.
1922	41	Concert tours and appreciation in England, Wales, France, Germany and Transylvania.	Foss (Lukas) born, Aug. 15; Pedrell (81) dies, Aug. 19; Xenakis born, May 1.
1923	42	Marriage with Ditta Pásztory; Dance Suite, and works by Dohnányi and Kodály, performed in celebration of jubilee of union of Pest and Buda.	Hlouschek born, Sept. 27.
1924	43	Publication of *Hungarian Folksong* (German edition, 1925); birth of son, Péter.	Busoni (58) dies, July 27; Fauré (79) dies, Nov. 4; Nono born, Jan. 29; Puccini (65) dies, Nov. 29; Stanford (71) dies, March 29.
1925	44	Recitals in Italy; success of Dance Suite at I.S.C.M. Festival at Prague.	Berio born, Boulez born, March 25; Satie (59) dies, July 1.
1926	45	*Miraculous Mandarin* and other works performed in Cologne.	Henze born, July 1; Zechlin (Ruth) born, June 22.
1927	46	Third String Quartet awarded prize in Philadelphia; first visit to U.S.A.	
1928	47	Fourth String Quartet for Pro Arte Quartet.	Janáček (74) dies, Aug. 12; Stockhausen born, Aug. 22.

YEAR	AGE	LIFE	CONTEMPORARY MUSICIANS
1929	48	Successful tour in U.S.S.R., and other concerts abroad.	
1930	49		Warlock (36) dies, Dec. 17.
1931	50	Performance of *Miraculous Mandarin* in honour of 50th birthday prevented by authorities; musician member of League of Nations Commission; Toldy Circle, Pressburg, reorganized as 'Béla Bartók Choral Society'—the first named after B.	d'Indy (80) dies, Dec. 2; Nielsen (66) dies, Oct. 2.
1932	51	Attendance at Folkmusic Congress in Cairo; period of illness.	d'Albert (67) dies, March 3.
1933	52	Première of Second Piano Concerto in Frankfurt—B.'s last performance in Germany.	Duparc (85) dies, Feb. 13; Karg-Elert (55) dies, April 9.
1934	53	Honour from Rumanian Government; released from piano teaching to concentrate on folksong research.	Delius (72) dies, June 10; Elgar (76) dies, Feb. 23; Holst (59) dies, May 25; Sekles (62) dies, Dec. 15.
1935	54	Première of Fifth String Quartet in Washington, D.C.	Berg (50) dies, Dec. 24; Dukas (69) dies, May 18; Loeffler (74) dies, May 19; Suk (61) dies, May 29.

YEAR	AGE	LIFE	CONTEMPORARY MUSICIANS
1936	55	Address to Hungarian Academy of Science; refusal of Greguss Prize; research in Turkey.	van Dieren (51) dies, April 24; Glazounov (70) dies, March 21; Respighi (56) dies, April 18.
1937	56	Music for Strings, Percussion and Celesta for Basel Philharmonic Orchestra; anger at German questionnaire concerning racial origins.	Gershwin (38) dies, July 11; Pierné (73) dies, July 17; Ravel (62) dies, Dec. 28; Roussel (68) dies, Aug. 23; Szymanowski (54) dies, March 29.
1938	57	First performance of Sonata for two pianos and percussion in Basel; anxiety after German occupation of Austria.	
1939	58	First performance of Violin Concerto in Amsterdam.	
1940	59	Tour of U.S.A. with Szigeti; final concert with wife in Budapest; arrival in New York, Oct. 29, as exiles; honorary doctorate and research assignment at Columbia University	
1941	60	Business affairs in confusion; deterioration in health.	Bridge (61) dies, Jan. 10; Walford Davies (71) dies, March 11; Distler (33) dies, Nov. 1.
1942	61	Symptoms of leukaemia evident.	Rakhmaninov (69) dies, March 28.

YEAR	AGE	LIFE	CONTEMPORARY MUSICIANS
1943	62	Last public appearance at New York Philharmonic Society concert, work on folksong continues and Concerto for Orchestra composed.	
1944	63	First performance of Concerto for Orchestra in Boston, and of Sonata for Solo Violin by Menuhin in New York; contract with Boosey & Hawkes.	Smyth (Ethel) (86) dies, May 8.
1945	64	B. dies in West Side Hospital, New York, Sept. 26.	Mascagni (81) dies, Aug. 2; Webern (61) dies, Sept. 15. Absil 52; Antheil 45; Armstrong (Louis) 45; Arnold 24; Asafiev 61; Auric 46; Bantock 77; Barber 35; Berio 20; Berkeley 42; Bernstein 27; Blacher 42; Bliss 54; Blitzstein 40; Bloch 65; Boulez 20; Brian (Havergal) 69; Britten 32; Bush 45; Cage 33; Casella 62; Castelnuovo-Tedesco 50; Copland 45; Cowell 48; Dallapiccola 41; Dessau 51; Dohnányi 68; Falla 69; Finzi 44; Fortner 38; Foss (Lukas) 23; Glière 70; Goossens 52; Grainger 63; Hamilton 23; Harris 47; Harsányi 47; Hauer 62; Henze 19; Hinde-

185

mith 50; Honegger 53; Ibert 55; Ives 71; Jongen 72; Kabalevsky 41; Kadosa 42; Kálmán 63; Kaminski (H.) 59; Khachaturian 42; Kodály 63; Krenek 45; Lehár 75; Malipiero 63; Martin 55; Medtner 65; Menotti 34; Messaien 37; Miaskovsky 64; Milhaud 53; Novák 75; Orff 50; Penderecki 12; Petrassi 41; Pfitzner 76; Piston 51; Pizzetti 65; Poulenc 56; Prokofiev 54; Rawsthorne 40; Rubbra 44; Ruggles 69; Schoenberg 71; Seiber 40; Sessions 49; Shostakovich 39; Sibelius 70; Skalkottas 41; Stockhausen 17; Strauss (R.) 71; Stravinsky 63; Turina 63; Varèse 60; Vaughan Williams 73; Veress 38; Villa-Lobos 58; Vlad 26; Weill 45; Wellesz 60.

Appendix B   Catalogue of Works

1 VOCAL WORKS

(A) VOICE AND PIANO

Three Songs   1898*
    (1) Im wunderschönen Monat Mai (Heine)
    (2) Nacht am Rheine (Siebel)
    (3) Ein Lied
Four Songs (Lajos Pósa)   1902
    (1) Őszi szellő—Autumn breeze
    (2) Még azt vetik a szememre—Thus they reproach me
    (3) Nincs olyan bú—There is no sorrow
    (4) Ejnye, ejnye—Oh! Oh!
Four Songs (MS lost)   1902*
Three popular songs (Sándor Peres, István Havas, Béla Sztankó)
    1904
Székely Folksong   1905
Five Songs   1905*
Hungarian Folksongs   1906 (rev. 1938)
    (a set of 20 in conjunction with Zoltán Kodály, the first 10
    being by Bartók)
    (1) Elindultam—Far behind I left my country
    (2) Általmennék—Crossing the river
    (3) Fehér László—The horse-thief
    (4) A gyulai—In the summer field
    (5) A kertmegi ert alatt—In a garden green
    (6) Ablakomba, ablakomba—Deceived in love
    (7) Száraz ágtól messze virít—Love's a burden

* Unpublished works.

(8) Végigmentem a tárkányi—Walking through the town
(9) Nem messze van innen Kismargitta—The horseman
(10) Szánt a babám—My love has gone a-ploughing

Ten Hungarian Folksongs 1906*
(continuation of previous)

Székely Folksongs 1907

Nine Rumanian Folksongs 1915*

Five Songs, Op. 15 1915–16
(Poems by Béla Balázs and others)
(1) Csókolni—Kiss
(2) Az én szerelmem—My love
(3) Színes álmomban—In vivid dreams
(4) Szomjasan vágyva várom—I wait with desire
(5) Itt lent a völgyben—In the valley

Five Songs (Endre Ady), Op. 16 1916
(1) Három őszi könnycsepp—Autumn tears
(2) Az őszi lárma—Autumn echoes
(3) Az ágyam hívogat—Lost content
(4) Egyedül a tengerrel—Alone with the sea
(5) Nem mehetek hozzád—I cannot come to you
(1st perf. Ilona Durigo, Bartók, Budapest, 21 April 1919)

Slovak Folksongs 1916

Eight Hungarian Folksongs 1907–17
(1) Fekete föld, fehér—The black earth is white
(2) Istenem, Istenem—My God, my God, make the river swell
(3) Asszonyok, asszonyok, had' legyek társatok—Women, women, let me join you
(4) Annyi bánat a szívemen—Such sorrow in my heart
(5) Ha kimegyek arra a magos tetőre—If I go out on that high roof
(6) Töltik a nagyerdő útját—They are mending the forest road
(7) Eddig való dolgom a tavaszi szántás—My work was ploughing in the spring
(8) Olvad a hó, csárdás kis angyalom—Snow is melting

Village Scenes 1924
 (five Slovak folksongs)
 (1) Szénagyüjtéskor—Hay-making
 (2) A menyasszonynál—At the bride's
 (3) Lakodalom—Wedding
 (4) Bölcsődal—Lullaby
 (5) Legénytánc—Lads' dance
 (1st perf. Mária Basilides, Bartók, Budapest, 8 December 1926)
Twenty Hungarian Folksongs 1929
 Vol. I Szomorú nóták—Songs of sorrow
 Vol. II Táncdalok—Dance songs
 Vol. III Vegyes dalok—Miscellaneous songs
 Vol. IV Új dalok—Songs in a new style
 (1st perf. M. Basilides, Bartók, Budapest, 30 January 1930)
Hungarian Folksong 1937
 arrangement of For Children, No. 16
Ukrainian Folksong 1945*
Goat Song 1945*

1 (B) VOICE AND ORCHESTRA

Five Songs, Op. 15 transcribed by Zoltán Kodály
Five Hungarian Folksongs (from Twenty Hungarian Folksongs, 1929) transcribed by Bartók

2 CHORAL WORKS

(A) FOR WOMEN'S OR CHILDREN'S VOICES

Two Rumanian Folksongs for 4 female voices, *a cappella* 1915*
Three Village Scenes 1926
 (nos. 3, 4, 5 of set of Five Slovak folksongs, 1924, see p. 121)
 for 4 or 8 female voices and chamber orchestra
 (1st perf. Budapest 1927)
Two- and three-part Songs 1935
 for female or children's voices, *a cappella*

Bartók

27 Songs in five volumes
Nos. 2, 8, 11, 12, 13, 16 arranged by Bartók for voices and orchestra
(1st perf. Budapest, 7 May 1938)

(B) FOR MEN'S VOICES

Evening (ed. D. Dille)   1903
   a cappella
Four Old Hungarian Folksongs   1910–12
   a cappella
    (1) Rég megmondtam, bús gerlice—Long ago I told you
    (2) Jaj istenem, kire várok—O God, who am I waiting for
    (3) Ángyomasszony kertje—In my sister-in-law's garden
    (4) Béreslegény, jól megrakd a szekeret—Boy, load the cart
       well
Five Slovak Folksongs   1917
   a cappella
    (1) Ej, posluchajte málo—Hey, my comrades
    (2) Ked'ja smutny podjem—If I must go to war
    (3) Kamarádi moj—My comrades
    (4) Ej, a ked'mna zabiju—Ah, if I fall
    (5) Ked's om siou na vojnu—I went forth to fight
    (1st perf. Vienna, 15 December 1917)
Six Székely Folksongs   1932
   a cappella
    (1) Hej, de sokszor megbántottál—How often you have
       grieved me
    (2) Istenem, életem—My God, my life
    (3) Vékony cérna, kemény mag—Slender thread, hard seed
    (4) Kilyénfalvi középtizbe—In Kilyénfalva girls assemble
    (5) Vékony cérna, kemény mag (see 3)
    (6) Járjad pap a táncot—Dance, priest
From Bygone Days   1935
   Three songs for male voices in 3 parts
   (1st perf. Budapest, 7 May 1937)

(C) FOR MIXED CHORUS

Two Songs 1904*
Four Slovak Folksongs 1917
    for mixed voices and piano
      (1) Zadala mamka—Wedding song from Poniky
      (2) Na holi, na holi—Song of the harvesters from Hiadel
      (3) Rada pila, rada jedla—Dance song from Medzibrod
      (4) Gajdujte, gajdence—Dance song from Poniky
      (1st perf. Budapest, 5 January 1917)
Four Hungarian Folksongs 1930
    a cappella
      (1) A rab—The prisoner
      (2) A bujdosó—The wanderer
      (3) Az eladó lány—Finding a husband
      (4) Dal—Song

(D) FOR SOLOISTS, CHORUS AND ORCHESTRA

Cantata Profana (The nine miraculous stags) 1930
    (text arranged by Bartók from traditional Rumanian folk
    ballads).
    For tenor and baritone solo, chorus and orchestra
    (1st perf. London, 25 May 1934)

3 WORKS FOR THE STAGE

[Duke] Bluebeard's Castle (Béla Balázs), Op. 11 1911
    Opera in one act
    (1st perf. Budapest, 24 May 1918)
The Wooden Prince (Béla Balázs), Op. 13 1916
    Ballet in one act
    (1st perf. Budapest, 12 May 1917)
The Miraculous Mandarin (Menyhért Lengyel), Op. 19 1919
    Pantomime in one act
    (1st perf. Cologne, 27 Nov. 1926)

4 CHAMBER MUSIC

Sonata for violin and piano   1894–7
Quartet for violin, viola, cello and piano   1898*
Quartet for 2 violins, viola and piano   1899*
Sonata for violin and piano   1903
    (1st perf. Budapest, 8 June 1903)
Quintet for 2 violins, viola, cello and piano   1904*
String Quartet No. 1, Op. 7   1908
    (1st perf. Waldbauer Quartet, Budapest, 19 Mar. 1910)
String Quartet No. 2, Op. 17   1915–17
    (1st perf. Waldbauer Quartet, Budapest, 3 Mar. 1918)
Sonata for violin and piano, No. 1   1921
    (1st perf. Jelly Arányi, Bartók, London, 22 Mar. 1922)
Sonata for violin and piano, No. 2   1922
    (1st perf. Jelly Arányi, Bartók, London, May 1923)
String Quartet No. 3   1927
    (1st perf. Waldbauer Quartet, Budapest, 6 Mar. 1929)
String Quartet No. 4   1928
    (1st perf. Waldbauer Quartet, Budapest, 20 Mar. 1929)
Rhapsody No. 1 for violin and piano   1928
    (1st perf. Joseph Szigeti, Bartók, Budapest, 22 Nov. 1929)
Rhapsody No. 2 for violin and piano   1928/1945
    (1st perf. Géza Frid, Bartók, Amsterdam, 19 Nov. 1928)
44 Duos for 2 violins   1931
String Quartet No. 5   1934
    (1st perf. Kolisch Quartet, Washington D.C., 8 Apr. 1935)
Sonata for Two Pianos and Percussion   1937
    (1st perf. Ditta and Béla Bartók, Basel, 16 Jan. 1938)
Contrasts for violin, clarinet and piano   1938
    (1st perf. Joseph Szigeti, Benny Goodman, Bartók, New
    York, 9 Jan. 1939)
String Quartet No. 6   1939
    (1st perf. Kolisch Quartet, New York, 20 Jan. 1941)
Sonata for solo violin   1944
    (ed. Yehudi Menuhin)
    (1st perf. Yehudi Menuhin, New York, 26 Nov. 1944)

5 PIANO SOLO

A Budapesti Torna Verseny, Gyorspolka   1890*
    Béla polka, *Katinka* (Gyorspolka)
    Jolán-polka, Nefelejts
The Course of the Danube   1891*
Three Pieces for the Piano   1894*
Introduction and Allegro, Walcer [*sic*],   1891–7*
    Tavaszi Dal, Fantasia, Sonata
Three Pieces for the Piano, Scherzo   1897
Evening   1903*
Four Piano Pieces   1903
    (1) Study for the left hand
    (2) Fantasia I
    (3) Fantasia II
    (4) Scherzo
    (1st perf. of 1, 4 and 2 or 3, Bartók, Berlin, 14 Dec. 1903)
Kossuth Symphony, Funeral march
    (last movement) from   1903
Rhapsody, Op. 1   1904
    (1st perf. Bartók, Bratislava, 4 Nov. 1904)
Three Folksongs from the County of Csík   1907
Fourteen Pieces for Piano, Op. 6   1908
    (in later editions described as Bagatelles)
    (1st perf. Bartók, Berlin, 1908)
Ten easy Pieces for Piano   1908
Two Elegies, Op. 8/b (formerly Op. 8/a)   1908–9
    (1st perf. Bartók, Budapest, 21 Apr. 1919)
For Children   1909/1945
    85 arrangements of folksongs in 4 volumes, of which the first
    two contain Hungarian and the last two Slovak tunes.
    In the revised edition of 1944 there are 79 items.
Two Rumanian Dances, Op. 8/a   1910
    (1st perf. Bartók, Paris, 12 Mar. 1910)
Sketches, Op. 9/b   1910
Four Dirges, Op. 9/a [formerly Op. 8/b]   1910
    (1st perf. E. von Dohnányi, Budapest, 17 Oct. 1917)

Bartók

Three Burlesques, Op. 8/c   1911
 (1st perf. E. von Dohnányi, Budapest, 17 Oct. 1917)
Allegro Barbaro   1911
 (1st perf. Bartók, Budapest, 27 Feb. 1921)
First Term at the Piano   1913
 18 pieces for beginners from the Sándor Reschofsky Piano
 School.
Oriental Dance   1913
Sonatina   1915
Rumanian Folksongs   1915
Rumanian Christmas Songs   1915
Suite, Op. 14   1916
 (1st perf. Bartók, Budapest, 21 Apr. 1919)
Fifteen Hungarian Folksongs   1917
 (Folksong arrangements originally intended for this collection
 but published later in a Paderewski memorial volume.)
Three Studies, Op. 18   1918
 (1st perf. Bartók, Budapest, 21 Apr. 1919)
Improvisations on Hungarian peasant songs, Op. 20   1920
 (1st perf. Bartók, Budapest, 27 Feb. 1921)
Sonata   1926
 (1st perf. Bartók, Budapest, 8 Dec. 1926)
Out of Doors   1926
 5 pieces in two volumes
 (1st perf. Bartók, Budapest, 8 Dec. 1926)
Nine little Piano Pieces   1926
 3 volumes
 (1st perf. Bartók, Budapest, 8 Dec. 1926)
Three Rondos on folk melodies   1926
Little Suite   1936
 arrangements of 5 pieces from 44 duos for 2 violins
Mikrokosmos   1926–39
 153 progressive studies in 6 volumes
Cadenzas for Mozart's Piano Concerto in E♭ major (K.365)
 1940*

6 ARRANGEMENTS BY BARTÓK

(A) FOR PIANO DUET, (B) FOR TWO PIANOS

(A)
The Miraculous Mandarin 1919
(B)
Rhapsody, Op. 1 1904
Suite No. 2, Op. 4 1907/41
Piano Concerto No. 1 1926
Piano Concerto No. 2 1930
Seven Pieces from *Mikrokosmos* 1937
Zipoli Suite 1945*

7 ORCHESTRAL WORKS

Symphony in E♭ major (lost) 1902*
    Scherzo of this work 1902*
Kossuth, Symphonic Poem 1903
    (1st perf. Budapest Philharmonic, Kerner, 13 Jan. 1904)
Rhapsody, Op. 1 1904
    arranged for piano and orchestra
    (1st perf. Bartók—Chevillard, Paris, Aug. 1905)
Scherzo, Op. 2 for piano and orchestra 1904
Suite No. 1, Op. 3 1905/20
    (1st perf. Ferdinand Löwe, Vienna, 29 Nov. 1905)
Suite No. 2, Op. 4 1907/20/43
    (1st perf.—incomplete—Berlin, 2 Jan. 1909; complete, Kerner, Budapest, 22 Nov. 1909)
Concerto No. 1 for violin and orchestra (posthumous) 1907–8
    (1st perf. W. Baumgarten—P. Sacher, Basel, May 1958)
Two Portraits 1907–8
    The first movement is identical with the first movement of the posthumous violin concerto; the transcription of the second for piano is identical with the last of the Fourteen Bagatelles.
Two Pictures, Op. 10 1910
    (1st perf. Budapest 25 Feb. 1913)

Rumanian Dance No. 1, Op. 8/a, arr. Bartók 1911
Four Orchestral Pieces, Op. 12 1912
    (1st perf. E. von Dohnányi, Budapest, 9 Jan. 1922)
Rumanian Folk Dances, arranged for orchestra from versions for
    piano 1915
The Wooden Prince, Op. 13 1916/31
    Suite for orchestra arr. Bartók
    (1st perf. E. von Dohnányi, Budapest, 23 Nov. 1931)
Fifteen Hungarian Peasant Songs 1917/1933
    transcribed for orchestra by Bartók
    (1st perf. Rotterdam, 18 Nov. 1933)
The Miraculous Mandarin, Op. 19 1919/23
    Concert Suite arr. Bartók
    (1st perf. Dresden, 1 July 1923)
Dance Suite 1923
    (1st perf. E. von Dohnányi, Budapest, 19 Nov. 1923)
Concerto No. 1 for piano and orchestra 1926
    (1st perf. Bartók—W. Furtwängler, Frankfurt/Main, 1 July
    1927)
Rhapsody No. 1 for violin and piano, arr. for violin and orchestra
    by Bartók 1928
Rhapsody No. 2 for violin and piano, arr. for violin and orchestra
    by Bartók 1928/45
    (1st perf. Zoltán Székely—P. Monteux, Amsterdam, Jan. 1932)
Concerto No. 2 for piano and orchestra 1930
    (1st perf. Bartók, Hans Rosbaud, Frankfurt/Main, 23 Jan.
    1933)
Dances from Transylvania 1931
    arrangement of Sonatina 1915
Hungarian Pictures 1931
    arrangement of various piano pieces
    (1st perf. Budapest, 26 Nov. 1934)
Music for Strings, Percussion and Celesta 1936
    (1st perf. P. Sacher, Basel Philharmonic, 21 Jan. 1937)
Concerto for two pianos and orchestra 1937/1940
    transcribed from Sonata for two pianos and percussion by
    Bartók

(1st perf. Louis Kentner, Ilona Kabos, Adrian Boult, London, 14 Nov. 1942)

Concerto No. 2 for violin and orchestra   1938
   (1st perf. Székely, Willem Mengelberg, Amsterdam, 23 Apr. 1939)

Divertimento for string orchestra   1939
   (1st perf. Sacher, Basel, 11 June 1940)

Concerto for Orchestra   1943
   (1st perf. Serge Koussevitzky, Boston Symphony Orchestra, 1 Dec. 1944)

Concerto for piano and orchestra No. 3   1945
   the last 17 bars were orchestrated by Tibor Serly
   (1st perf. György Sándor, E. Ormandy, Philadelphia, 8 Feb. 1946)

Concerto for viola and orchestra   1945
   This work was assembled from sketches and memoranda by Tibor Serly, who also orchestrated it.
   (1st perf. William Primrose, A. Doráti, Minneapolis, 2 Dec. 1949)

This Catalogue does not include the large number of arrangements of movements from Bartók's works by other hands.

Appendix C   Personalia

Ady, Endre (1877–1919), Hungarian writer, came from a minor aristocratic family. Inspired by early experiences in provincial journalism and by visits to Paris, he campaigned with his pen for an independent and democratic Hungary, freed from its feudal trappings. Ady was a poet of genius who had little liking for empty literary convention and restored ancient practices of Hungarian versification. He was one of the founders of the journal *Nyugat* (*West*) and exerted a strong influence on progressive Hungarian artists of all kinds.

Arányi, Jelly (1893–1966), younger sister of the violinist Adila Arányi (Fachiri), was a great-niece of Joachim and herself a distinguished violinist. She was a pupil of Hubay (q.v.) in Budapest. Bartók dedicated two violin sonatas to Jelly Arányi, who was also the dedicatee of Ravel's *Tsigane* for violin and orchestra. After 1923 she lived in England, where she gave memorable performances of Vaughan Williams's *The Lark ascending* and *Concerto accademico*.

Backhaus, Wilhelm (1884–1969), born and educated in Leipzig, became a teacher of piano at the Royal Manchester College of Music in 1905. At the same time he developed his interpretative gifts to the point at which he was recognized as one of the notable virtuosi of the twentieth century. He eventually settled in Switzerland.

Balázs, Béla (1884–1949), a well-known poet and pioneer of film aesthetics, was the author of the libretto of Bartók's first opera, *Duke Bluebeard's Castle* (see p. 85) and of the ballet *The Wooden Prince* (see p. 98). Balázs was also friendly with Kodály, who set a number of his poems to music.

Beu, Octavian (b. 1893), a Rumanian folklore scholar with whom Bartók discussed subjects of mutual interest, often in their wider context.

Bihari, János (1764–1827), Hungarian violinist of gipsy origin of remarkable skill. His province was that of folk-music and he was the master of the *verbunkos*. His playing made a deep impression on Liszt.

Bodon, Pál (1884–1953), friend of Bartók and in later life Director of the Music School in Kecskemét.

Buşiţia, János (1876–1953), schoolmaster at Belényes in Rumania, helped Bartók with his researches into Rumanian folksong. Bartók held Buşitia in the highest esteem and the letters written by him to Buşiţia are some of the most eloquent and informative that he ever wrote. A number of these letters are preserved in the Bartók Archives in Budapest.

Carreño, Teresa (1853–1917), Venezuelan pianist, born in Caracas, who studied in New York and Paris. She not only lived the life of a virtuoso pianist but also undertook the career of an opera singer. She had four husbands, of whom Eugen d'Albert (1864–1932) was the third.

Dent, Edward Joseph (1876–1957), a Yorkshireman, was Professor of Music, Cambridge University, from 1926 until 1941. Dent was the best-known musical scholar of his period, distinguished alike for his contributions to musicology, his talent for teaching, his practical endeavours in the field of opera, his mastery of European languages and his diplomacy. Dent, whose creative output included a few musical compositions, helped to found the International Society for Contemporary Music, of which he was president until 1938.

Foulds, John (1880–1939), a native of Manchester, was a member of the Hallé Orchestra. A protégé of Hans Richter, with whom he travelled abroad and for whom he occasionally conducted concerts, he resigned from the orchestra in 1906 to devote himself to composition and conducting.

Geyer, Stefi (1888–1956), a brilliant Hungarian violinist, sometime a pupil of Hubay (q.v.), who made her home in Zürich and married the Swiss composer Walter Schulthess in 1920.

Bartók wrote frequently to Stefi Geyer, for whom his feelings were notably warm, and to her husband. Correspondence between him and the Schulthesses (1928–40) is preserved in the Bartók Archives, New York.

Godowsky, Leopold (1870–1938), a Polish-born pianist, settled in the U.S.A. in 1901. He was at that time Director of a Conservatory in Chicago. Between 1909 and 1914 he taught in Vienna. A naturalized American citizen, he ended his life in New York.

Gray, Cecil (1895–1951), Anglo-Scottish critic and writer on musical subjects. Gray provoked many by the unconventionality of his views, his disregard of established eminence and the flavour of his distinctive prose style. A friend of Philip Heseltine (q.v.), whose biography he wrote, Gray helped him to found the short-lived journal *The Sackbut*.

Gruber, Emma (?1868–1958), *née* Sándor, was one of the famous hostesses of Budapest at the turn of the century. Her brother was a prominent politician, her first husband a business man and an amateur violinist. Mrs Gruber was herself a competent practising musician with a flair for composition, but she chiefly devoted herself to the encouragement of the talents of those who were less well circumstanced but more talented. Bartók dedicated to her his first Fantasy for piano (1903) and his Rhapsody (Op. 1, 1904). In 1910 she became the wife of Zoltán Kodály.

Herzfeld, Viktor (1856–1920), composer, conductor and professor of theory at the Academy of Music in Budapest. Herzfeld, a regular member of the circle of musicians and intellectuals associated with Mrs Gruber, retired from his professorship in 1907 and was succeeded by Zoltán Kodály.

Heseltine, Philip (known as Warlock, Peter) (1894–1930), English musical scholar and composer, known for his editing and championship of music of the seventeenth century and for his songs. Heseltine, whose enthusiasm for Delius complemented his antiquarian studies, visited Budapest in 1921. There he met both Bartók and Kodály. The former was Heseltine's guest in Wales in 1922.

Hubay, Jenő von (1858–1938), born in Budapest, was an infant prodigy violinist and a pupil of Joachim. He became an outstanding teacher and a whole generation of distinguished Hungarian violinists owed much to his tuition. He was also a composer, but his cautious conservatism led him to view Bartók's music with disfavour. He was director of the Academy of Music from 1919 until 1934.

Kerner, István (1867–1929), a famous Hungarian conductor who directed the first Budapest performance of Bartók's *Kossuth* Symphony in 1904. In the same year he conducted a performance of Elgar's *In the South* in Budapest.

Kisfaludy, Károly (1788–1830), brother of Sándor Kisfaludy (1772–1844), a great national poet, was the first outstanding Hungarian Romantic writer. After army service he lived in Vienna, at first intending to become a painter. Literature and drama, however, claimed him and his romantic comedies became landmarks in the history of Hungarian theatre. Kisfaludy founded an 'Aurora' Society, which was a magnet for young writers. In 1844 the ideals of this society were incorporated into the Kisfaludy Society, which, among other things, busied itself with the collection of folk-poetry.

Kodály, Zoltán (1882–1967), an outstanding Hungarian musician who was equally distinguished as scholar, composer and educationalist. Kodály, whose *Psalmus Hungaricus* is almost a national anthem, laid the foundations of the present musical education system in Hungary. A great friend of Bartók, with whom he worked closely in the field of folksong research, he was better able to meet the challenges of changing political circumstances. He remained in his native country through many vicissitudes and in the last years of his life was recognized by his fellow countrymen as the greatest among them.

Koessler, Hans (1853–1926), a German and cousin to Max Reger, was the senior professor of composition at the Budapest Academy of Music. He was a stern disciplinarian and was displeased at any deviation from the line of Brahmsian rectitude on the part of his pupils. Among these were Bartók, Dohnányi, Kodály and Weiner.

Láng, Paul Henry (b. 1901), musicologist, was born and educated in Budapest. He later studied in Paris and in the U.S.A., where he settled. In 1933 he was appointed professor at Columbia University, New York, since when he has written a large number of works distinguished by a breadth of sympathy and knowledge.

Lengyel, Menyhért (b. 1880), a Hungarian playwright who belonged to the naturalistic group led by Ferenc Molnár and associated with the Gay Theatre, Budapest. Lengyel's 'grotesque pantomime' *The Miraculous Mandarin* (in Bartók's setting only allowed performance in Budapest after Bartók's death) was published in the famous literary journal *Nyugat* (see under Ady, Endre, p. 198) in 1917. He later emigrated to the U.S.A.

Mihalovich, Ödön (1842–1929), successor to Ferenc Erkel as Director of the Academy of Music in Budapest, was successful in persuading the authorities to provide a building worthy of the reputation of the Academy. Mihalovich was a busy composer whose reputation in that field died with him.

Pásztory, Ditta (b. 1903), Hungarian pianist, was first Bartók's pupil and then his second wife. She appeared with her husband many times in recitals of music for two pianos. After Bartók's death she returned to Budapest.

Pósa, Lajos (1850–1914), Hungarian poet, four of whose poems were set to music by Bartók. Pósa wrote much poetry for children and enjoyed a considerable degree of popularity.

Prunières, Henry (1886–1942), French musicologist, was a pupil at the Sorbonne of Romain Rolland. His published works include studies of Lully and Monteverdi. In 1920 Prunières founded the journal *La Revue musicale*.

Reinitz, Béla (1878–1943), composer and critic, who was among the first to praise Bartók's music in Budapest. To him Bartók dedicated his settings of poems by Endre Ady (q.v.), since Reinitz himself was best known for his eloquent settings of Ady's poems. During the brief period of revolutionary government in 1918–19 Reinitz was in charge of the organization of musical life in Hungary.

Richter, Hans (1843–1916), a conductor of Hungarian origin who became Wagner's assistant and a notable interpreter of Wagner's music dramas. Richter built up a massive reputation and was regarded as the greatest conductor of his generation. At various times he held appointments in Vienna, Munich, Brussels, Bayreuth, London, Manchester and Birmingham. Richter made possible Bartók's first appearance in England. He was also responsible for establishing Elgar's reputation.

Sauer, Emil von (1862–1942), born in Hamburg, was a pupil of Liszt. From the age of twenty he led the life of a peripatetic virtuoso, becoming a familiar figure in the concert halls of Europe. He began to visit Budapest in 1890 and thereafter frequently performed there. In 1901 he was appointed principal piano professor at the Vienna Conservatory.

Schiffer, Adolf (1875–1950), well-known cellist and pupil of David Popper (1843–1913), German-Czech professor of cello in Budapest from 1896.

Schuch, Ernst von (1846–1914), Austrian-born conductor, who became Court Music Director in Dresden in 1873 after having served a year as conductor. Schuch was responsible for notable performances of the early operas of Richard Strauss.

Stravinsky, Igor (1882–1971), Russian born but resident for long periods in France and the U.S.A., was the most brilliant musical personality of the first half of the twentieth century. Bartók greatly admired the famous works composed by Stravinsky before the First World War, but was not impressed by Stravinsky's views on the abstractness of music.

Székely, Zoltán (b. 1903), Hungarian violinist and composer, studied in Budapest with Hubay and Kodály. From the early 1920s he lived in Holland. In 1935 Székely formed the Hungarian String Quartet. Bartók dedicated his second Rhapsody for violin and piano to Székely, for whom he also composed the Second Violin Concerto.

Szigeti, Jozseph (1892–1973), Hungarian-born violinist, pupil of Hubay, who made his career abroad, especially in Switzerland and the U.S.A. Bartók gave recitals with Szigeti, to whom he dedicated his first Rhapsody for violin and piano. *Contrasts for Violin, Clarinet and Pianoforte* was dedicated to Szigeti and the American clarinet-player Benny Goodman.

Szymanowski, Karol (1882–1937) was the most important Polish composer of the first part of the twentieth century. During the First World War he lived as an exile in Russia. In 1922 he became professor of composition and director of the State Conservatory in Warsaw.

Tango, Egisto (1873–1951), Italian conductor, was musical director of the Budapest Opera from 1912 to 1919. In gratitude for Tango's efforts on behalf of the work Bartók dedicated *The Wooden Prince* to him.

Thomán, István (1862–1941), Hungarian pianist, was a pupil of Liszt. He became the principal piano-teacher in the Academy of Music in Budapest, where Bartók and Dohnányi were among his pupils. He showed much solicitude for the young Bartók in every way. In 1903 Bartók dedicated to him his *Study for the left hand*.

Vécsey, Ferenc von (1893–1935), a 'wonder-child' violinist and pupil of Hubay and Joachim. In 1906 Bartók travelled with him as accompanist through Spain and Portugal.

Waldbauer, Imre (1892–1952), a violin pupil of Hubay, was a professor of violin at the Academy of Music, Budapest. He founded the string quartet that bore his name and with it helped to make the reputation of many Hungarian composers, among them Bartók and Kodály. In the last part of his life he lived in the U.S.A.

Appendix D   Bibliography

Bartók, Béla, *Hungarian Folksong* (Budapest, 1924).* English translation, 1931.

Our Folk-music and that of the Neighbouring Peoples (Budapest, 1934).*

Collected Writings on Music (Budapest, 1948).*

'La Musique hongroise' in *Revue musicale* (Paris, 1920).

'Neue Ergebnisse der Volksliedforschung in Ungarn' in *Musikblätter des Anbruchs* (Vienna, 1932).

'Hungarian Peasant Music' in *Musical Quarterly* (New York, 1933).

'Gypsy Music or Hungarian Music?' in *Ethnographia,* 1931 and *Musical Quarterly* (New York, 1947).

'Folksong Research in Eastern Europe' in *Musical America* (New York, 1943).

Béla Bartók—A Memorial Review, containing a number of articles by Bartók (New York, 1950).

Bator, Victor, 'The Béla Bartók Archives [in New York]' (New York, 1963).

Bónis, F., *Béla Bartók, his Life in Pictures* (Budapest/London, 1964).

Breuer, J., 'On Three Posthumous Editions of Works by Bartók' in *Studia Musicologica Academiae Scientarum Hungaricae,* Vol. 13 (Budapest, 1971).

Demény, János, *Béla Bartók, Letters, Photographs, Mss. etc.* (Budapest, 1948).*

Béla Bartók's Letters, collected and edited (Budapest, 1951, 1955).*

Béla Bartók, Letters (London, 1971).

* In Hungarian.

'Béla Bartók's Student Years and Romantic Period' in *Musical Dissertations II* (Budapest, 1954).*

'The Years of the Artistic Development of Béla Bartók' in *Musical Dissertations III* (Budapest, 1955).*

Dille, D., *Béla Bartók* (Brussels, 1947).

'Documenta Bartókiana [in the Bartók Archives, Budapest]' (Budapest, 1964–).*

Engelmann, Hans Ulrich, *Béla Bartók's Mikrokosmos* (Würzburg, 1953).

Finkelstein, Sidney, *Art and Society* (New York, 1947).

Foulds, John, *Music Today* (London, 1934).

Gerson-Kiwi, E., 'Béla Bartók—Scholar in Folk Music' in *Music and Letters* (London, 1957).

Haraszti, Emil, *Béla Bartók: his Life and Works* (Paris, 1938).

Béla Bartók (Paris, 1949).

Kodály, Zoltán, *Folk Music of Hungary* (Budapest, 1937;* in translation, London, 1960).

'Béla Bartók the Man' in *Új Zenei Szemle* I, no. 1 (Budapest, 1947).*

Molnár, Antal, 'Contributions towards a biography of Bartók' in *Új Zenei Szemle* I, no. 1 (Budapest, 1947).*

Matzon-Somos, *Establishment and Activity of the Béla Bartók Choral Society in Pozsony* (Pressburg) (Pozsony, 1942).*

Moreux, Serge, *Béla Bartók, Sa vie—Ses œuvres—Son langage* (Paris, 1949).

Nüll, Edwin von der, *Béla Bartók: ein Beitrag zur Morphologie der neuen Musik* (Halle/Saale, 1930).

Saygan, A. A., 'Bartók in Turkey' in *Musical Quarterly* (New York, 1951).

Schreyer, Victor, Monograph on the traditions of Nagyszentmiklós (Nagyszentmiklós, 1912).*

Seiber, Mátyás, *The String Quartets of Béla Bartók* (London & New York, 1945).

Stevens, Halsey, *The Life and Music of Béla Bartók* (New York & Oxford, 1953, 2nd ed. 1964).

Suchoff, Benjamin, 'Béla Bartók's Contributions to Music Education' in *Tempo* (London, 1962).

Szabolcsi, Bence, *Romantic Hungarian Music of the Nineteenth Century* (Budapest, 1951).*
'The Miraculous Mandarin' in *Musical Dissertations III* (Budapest, 1955).*
Béla Bartók (with illustrations documented by F. Bónis, letters of Bartók selected by J. Demény, and discography by L. Somfai) (Leipzig, 1968).
Szervánszky, Endre, 'Who studies the Works of Bartók' in *Zenepedagógia* II, nos. 2 & 4 (Budapest).*
Uhde, Jürgen, *Bartók—Mikrokosmos* (Regensburg, 1955).
Ujfalussy, József, *Béla Bartók*, 2 vols (Budapest, 1965).*

Programmes of the Royal Pressburg Grammar School (1893–1899),* the Béla Bartók Choral Society of Bratislava (1941),* and the International Béla Bartók Choral Competition (Debrecen, 1961).*

Various articles on Bartók in English have appeared in *The New Hungarian Quarterly* as follows: Issues 4 (1961), 6 (1962), 11 (1963), 17 (1965), 24 (1966), 39 (1970), 40 (1970).

Béla Bartók's Ethnomusikologische Schriften (in facsimile, ed. D. Dille) are in process of appearing progressively from Editio Musica (Budapest) and B. Schott's Söhne (Mainz), while *Das Gesamtwerk auf Schallplatten* is also appearing progressively from Bärenreiter-Verlag (Kassel).

Appendix E   The *Kossuth* Symphony: Notice in *The Manchester Guardian*, 19th February 1904

In the Symphonic Poem 'Kossuth', which was the principal unfamiliar work played at yesterday's concert, Mr Béla Bartók declares himself an uncompromising disciple of the later Strauss, as a musician. His Hungarian patriotism appears in his choice of a subject, but not at all in his musical procedure. Of the national Hungarian melodies which have inspired so many eminent composers—in particular Schubert, Liszt, and Brahms—he shows no consciousness whatever in the course of his elaborate and ambitious orchestral poem. In fact the only previously existing theme to which reference is made is the Austrian National Anthem, commonly known as 'Haydn's Hymn to the Emperor'. As to the manner in which that is used we shall have something to say in the sequel.

The suggestions of Strauss and in particular of Strauss's 'Heldenleben' are too various and too strong to be accidental. Even the constitution of the orchestra, with eight horns, two harps, and one or more additional tubas, is Straussian. In the preliminary characterisation of the hero the procedure is exactly the same as in 'Heldenleben', though there is no trace of resemblance in the thematic material. Passing to the dialogue between Kossuth and his wife we are reminded of the 'Hero's Companion', whose voice takes the form of a recurrent violin solo in the Strauss composition. Then comes the battle, quite as ugly as Strauss's, and open to one definite charge of a kind that cannot be brought against Strauss—the charge, namely, that the travesty of the 'Austrian Hymn' is ferocious and hideous. There is nothing in precise correspondence with the section called by Strauss 'The Hero's Works of Peace', Mr Bartók's composition ending with the patriotic lamentations of a surviving remnant. It is, however, clear that the young Hungarian composer has been very strongly influenced by Strauss both in the fundamental conception of his Symphonic Poem and in his manner of putting it together. There is a slight hint even of Strauss's peculiar vein of musical invention in the dialogue between Kossuth and his wife, but for the rest the detail of the invention seems to be original enough.

Other first impressions we can only indicate briefly. The mere fact that a young composer should attempt to follow in the footsteps of so tremendous a 'Jack the Giant-Killer' as Strauss would seem to betray the consciousness of great powers, and the degree of facility in handling great orchestral masses exhibited by Mr Bartók would be remarkable in anyone, and is doubly surprising in so young an artist. His themes, too, have life in them, and in certain cases awaken a hope that in course of time, when he shall have had enough of the Straussian goose-chase, he may do excellent work. We would, however, suggest that, though the imitation of Strauss's 'Heldenleben' extravagances is a mistake into which only a young man of very great talent would be likely to fall, it is nevertheless a very bad mistake. In the music of mood-painting and graphic suggestion the worst and most frequent fault is the attempt to bring too much within the scope of a single composition.

The great difference between the earlier and later Strauss is that the former takes a comparatively broad and simple subject and gives his musical symbols time to develop and convey their message intelligibly, whereas the latter gives up all attempt to make his music independently intelligible, crowds his score with incongruous detail, and multiplies explanations in the programme with the growing consciousness that the music alone misses fire. This is a general objection to the procedure of the later Strauss. To such 'battle' sections as that which Mr Bartók, under the obvious influence of Strauss, has composed there is a more special objection. No great luck has hitherto attended representations of fighting in music. Beethoven's 'Battle Symphony' is the only symphonic work by that master which later generations have agreed to neglect. Tchaikovsky's '1812' Overture—a piece of the same kind—is admitted by all experts to be his worst composition. As to the battle scene in Strauss's 'Heldenleben', it has gone far towards undermining that gifted composer's reputation. It probably represents the worst blunder ever committed by a composer of genius.

Nor is it difficult to understand why composers fail in such an undertaking. A battle suggests to the imagination a greater variety of violent and ugly sounds than any other scene, and great variety in ugliness does not produce beauty; nor do unresolved discords on eight horns, four trombones, and two tubas sound better than the same unresolved discords on a pianoforte. The nearest approach to a successful battle picture in music occurs in the first movement of Tchaikovsky's Sixth Symphony, where the word 'picture' is not quite in place, because the composer does not attempt to suggest external things, but only the mood evoked by them. Of such pictures in general the proverbial 'Battle of Prague' may be taken as typical.

The mention of Tchaikovsky reminds us of another special point in the 'Kossuth' Symphony. No justification of any kind can be found for such use as Mr Bartók's of the Austrian Hymn. It cannot be pretended that the strains of that noble anthem have any fitness for the musical purpose. They form a mere label, informing the listener that the reference is here to the Austrian host. Moreover the guying and degrading of the famous melody is altogether repulsive. Tchaikovsky made a similar mistake in the '1812' Overture representing the Russians by the national anthem of the present day, 'Bozhe, Tsarya khrani', which had not been composed in 1812, and the French by the 'Marseillaise', typical of a regime that was not in power when the French invaded Russia. Historically therefore, as well as musically, the use of both those melodies is perfectly inept, and is on a par with the persistent references in 'Charley's Aunt' to Brazil as the place 'where the nuts come from'. It is only the musical objection to which Mr Bartók's use of the Austrian Hymn is open. Apart from the function of the theme as a barefaced label, analogous to a piece of writing in the middle of a painted picture, 'Yankee Doodle' would have answered the purpose much better. The best part of the composition is the patriotic lament at the end. The rendering of the elaborate score yesterday showed the most careful and conscientious preparation. The performance was received with a fair amount of applause, which the composer acknowledged. If anyone thinks, however, that it really pleased the Manchester public he is under a very gross delusion.

As a pianist Mr Bartók displayed powers of a less exceptional kind, but he was more satisfactory on the whole. Liszt's 'Spanish Rhapsody' becomes, with the help of Busoni's orchestration, a gorgeous piece of Carnival music. The solo part Mr Bartók played with technical power fully equal to all its demands, and his rendering did not lack geniality and charm. He afterwards gave two pieces without accompaniment—a very peculiar set of modern Variations, by Volkmann, on the theme of Handel's harpsichord piece 'The Harmonious Blacksmith', that scarcely seemed to justify its existence, and secondly, in answer to an encore, a Scherzo of his own, showing some of the same tendency to harmonic extravagance as his orchestral piece, but piquant in rhythm and stamped with genuine if somewhat eccentric talent.

The music of the old order was represented at this concert by Schubert's 'Unfinished Symphony', of which a finely inspired and technically faultless interpretation was given. The reception showed how genuine a place this most typically Schubertian of all orchestral pieces has in the affections of the Hallé audience. Dvořák's lighthearted and graceful Suite at the end afforded welcome relief from the music, more or less affected by eccentricity and recklessness, which occupied the middle parts of the programme.

(This notice was probably by Arthur Johnstone [1861–1904] who was described by Elgar as '. . . *the* best critic we had'.)

Index

Index

Index

Index